# Illustrated Novell NetWare 2.15

Timothy K. McDonald

Wordware Publishing, Inc.

**Library of Congress Cataloging-in-Publication Data**
McDonald, Timothy
Illustrated Novell NetWare 2.15 / Timothy K. McDonald.
p. cm.
Includes index.
ISBN 1-55622-191-6
1. NetWare (Computer operating system). I. Title.
QA76.76.O63M39 1990
005.7'1369—dc20 90-12900
CIP

Copyright © 1991 Wordware Publishing, Inc.

All Rights Reserved

1506 Capital Ave.
Plano, Texas 75074

No part of this book may be reproduced in any form or by any means without permission in writing from Wordware Publishing, Inc.

Printed in the United States of America

ISBN 1-55622-191-6

10 9 8 7 6 5 4 3 2 1

V9008

NetWare, Novell, SFT, TTS, and ELS are registered trademarks of Novell, Inc.
IBM, PC AT, PC XT, PS/2, and PC-DOS are registered trademarks of International Business Machines Corporation.
Compaq, DeskPro, DeskPro 286, and DeskPro 386 are registered trademarks of Compaq Computer Corporation.
AT&T and AT&T 6300 are registered trademarks of AT&T Bell Laboratories.
Microsoft and MS-DOS are registered trademarks of Microsoft Corporation.
ARCnet is a registered trademark of Datapoint Corporation.
ETHERNET is a registered trademark of Xerox Corporation.
All other trademarks are of their respective manufacturers.

All inquiries for volume purchases of this book should be addressed to Wordware Publishing, Inc. at the above address. Telephone inquiries may be made by calling:

(214) 423-0090

# Contents


| Module | Title | Page |
|---|---|---|
| 1 | About This Book | 1 |
| 2 | An Overview of a Novell Network | 3 |
| 3 | Hardware Installation | 11 |
| 4 | COMPSURF | 13 |
| 5 | NET$OS | 17 |
| 6 | INSTALL | 19 |
| 7 | START | 24 |
| 8 | Workstation Shells (ANET and NET) | 27 |
| 9 | Troubleshooting | 29 |
| 10 | Booting the System | 31 |
| 11 | ARCHIVE | 35 |
| 12 | ATOTAL | 39 |
| 13 | ATTACH | 40 |
| 14 | BINDFIX | 41 |
| 15 | BINDREST | 43 |
| 16 | BROADCAST | 44 |
| 17 | CAPTURE | 45 |
| 18 | CASTOFF | 50 |
| 19 | CASTON | 52 |
| 20 | CHANGE QUEUE | 54 |
| 21 | CHKVOL | 55 |
| 22 | CLEAR MESSAGE | 56 |
| 23 | CLEAR STATION | 57 |
| 24 | CONFIG | 58 |
| 25 | CONSOLE | 59 |
| 26 | CPMOFF | 60 |
| 27 | CPMON | 61 |
| 28 | DISABLE LOGIN | 62 |
| 29 | DISK | 63 |
| 30 | DISMOUNT | 65 |
| 31 | DOS | 66 |
| 32 | DOWN | 67 |
| 33 | ENABLE LOGIN | 69 |
| 34 | ENDCAP | 70 |
| 35 | ENDSPOOL | 72 |
| 36 | EOJOFF | 74 |
| 37 | EOJON | 75 |

# Contents (Continued)


| Module | Title | Page |
|---|---|---|
| 38 | FCONSOLE | 76 |
| 39 | FILER | 79 |
| 40 | FLAG | 85 |
| 41 | FORM CHECK | 87 |
| 42 | FORM SET | 88 |
| 43 | GRANT | 89 |
| 44 | HELP | 91 |
| 45 | HIDEFILE | 94 |
| 46 | HOLDOFF | 96 |
| 47 | HOLDON | 97 |
| 48 | KILL PRINTER | 98 |
| 49 | KILL QUEUE | 99 |
| 50 | LISTDIR | 100 |
| 51 | LOGIN | 102 |
| 52 | LOGIN SCRIPTS | 104 |
| 53 | LOGOUT | 109 |
| 54 | MAIL | 110 |
| 55 | MAKEUSER | 115 |
| 56 | MAP | 119 |
| 57 | MENU | 122 |
| 58 | MONITOR | 125 |
| 59 | MOUNT | 127 |
| 60 | NAME | 128 |
| 61 | NCOPY | 129 |
| 62 | NDIR | 130 |
| 63 | NPRINT | 133 |
| 64 | NSNIPES | 137 |
| 65 | OFF | 139 |
| 66 | PAUDIT | 140 |
| 67 | PCONSOLE | 141 |
| 68 | PRINTCON | 144 |
| 69 | PRINTDEF | 148 |
| 70 | PRINTER | 151 |
| 71 | PSTAT | 155 |
| 72 | PURGE | 157 |
| 73 | QUEUE (CONSOLE 2.1) | 159 |
| 74 | QUEUE (CONSOLE) | 160 |

# Contents (Continued)


| Module | Title | Page |
|---|---|---|
| 75 | QUEUE (PUBLIC) | 162 |
| 76 | REMOVE | 165 |
| 77 | RENDIR | 166 |
| 78 | REROUTE PRINTER | 168 |
| 79 | REVOKE | 170 |
| 80 | REWIND PRINTER | 172 |
| 81 | RIGHTS | 174 |
| 82 | SALVAGE | 176 |
| 83 | SECURITY | 178 |
| 84 | SEND (CONSOLE) | 180 |
| 85 | SEND (PUBLIC) | 181 |
| 86 | SESSION | 183 |
| 87 | SET TIME | 186 |
| 88 | SETPASS | 187 |
| 89 | SHOWFILE | 189 |
| 90 | SLIST | 190 |
| 91 | SMODE | 191 |
| 92 | SPOOL | 193 |
| 93 | START PRINTER | 198 |
| 94 | STOP PRINTER | 199 |
| 95 | SYSCON | 200 |
| 96 | SYSTIME | 203 |
| 97 | TIME | 204 |
| 98 | TLIST | 205 |
| 99 | UDIR | 207 |
| 100 | USERLIST | 209 |
| 101 | VOLINFO | 211 |
| 102 | WHOAMI | 213 |
| Appendix A | Terms and Definitions | 215 |
| Appendix B | Novell Commands and Syntax | 219 |
| Appendix C | Novell NetWare Exercises | 222 |
| Appendix D | NetWare 386 | 232 |
| Index | | 241 |

# Recommended Learning Sequence



| Sequence | | Description | Module | Page |
|---|---|---|---|---|
| □ | 1 | About This Book | 1 | 1 |
| □ | 2 | An Overview of a Novell Network | 2 | 3 |
| □ | 3 | Hardware Installation | 3 | 11 |
| □ | 4 | COMPSURF | 4 | 13 |
| □ | 5 | NET$OS | 5 | 17 |
| □ | 6 | INSTALL | 6 | 19 |
| □ | 7 | START | 7 | 24 |
| □ | 8 | Workstation Shells (ANET and NET) | 8 | 27 |
| □ | 9 | Troubleshooting | 9 | 29 |
| □ | 10 | Booting the System | 10 | 31 |
| □ | 11 | LOGIN | 51 | 102 |
| □ | 12 | LOGOUT | 53 | 109 |
| □ | 13 | SLIST | 90 | 190 |
| □ | 14 | ATTACH | 13 | 40 |
| □ | 15 | HELP | 44 | 91 |
| □ | 16 | SETPASS | 88 | 187 |
| □ | 17 | WHOAMI | 102 | 213 |
| □ | 18 | USERLIST | 100 | 209 |
| □ | 19 | SEND (PUBLIC) | 85 | 181 |
| □ | 20 | CASTOFF | 18 | 50 |
| □ | 21 | CASTON | 19 | 52 |
| □ | 22 | SYSTIME | 96 | 203 |
| □ | 23 | VOLINFO | 101 | 211 |
| □ | 24 | CHKVOL | 21 | 55 |
| □ | 25 | RIGHTS | 81 | 174 |
| □ | 26 | GRANT | 43 | 89 |
| □ | 27 | TLIST | 98 | 205 |
| □ | 28 | REVOKE | 79 | 170 |
| □ | 29 | REMOVE | 76 | 165 |
| □ | 30 | FLAG | 40 | 85 |
| □ | 31 | NDIR | 62 | 130 |
| □ | 32 | UDIR | 99 | 207 |
| □ | 33 | LISTDIR | 50 | 100 |
| □ | 34 | RENDIR | 77 | 166 |
| □ | 35 | MAP | 56 | 119 |
| □ | 36 | SMODE | 91 | 191 |

# Recommended Learning Sequence (Cont.)

| Sequence | | Description | Module | Page |
|---|---|---|---|---|
| □ | 37 | NCOPY | 61 | 129 |
| □ | 38 | SALVAGE | 82 | 176 |
| □ | 39 | PURGE | 72 | 157 |
| □ | 40 | CAPTURE | 17 | 45 |
| □ | 41 | ENDCAP | 34 | 70 |
| □ | 42 | ENDSPOOL | 35 | 72 |
| □ | 43 | NPRINT | 63 | 133 |
| □ | 44 | PRINTCON | 68 | 144 |
| □ | 45 | PRINTDEF | 69 | 148 |
| □ | 46 | PSTAT | 71 | 155 |
| □ | 47 | PCONSOLE | 67 | 141 |
| □ | 48 | QUEUE (PUBLIC) | 75 | 162 |
| □ | 49 | NSNIPES | 64 | 137 |
| □ | 50 | CPMOFF | 26 | 60 |
| □ | 51 | CPMON | 27 | 61 |
| □ | 52 | EOJOFF | 36 | 74 |
| □ | 53 | EOJON | 37 | 75 |
| □ | 54 | HOLDON | 47 | 97 |
| □ | 55 | HOLDOFF | 46 | 96 |
| □ | 56 | HIDEFILE | 45 | 94 |
| □ | 57 | SHOWFILE | 89 | 189 |
| □ | 58 | FCONSOLE | 38 | 76 |
| □ | 59 | LOGIN SCRIPTS | 52 | 104 |
| □ | 60 | SYSCON | 95 | 200 |
| □ | 61 | MAKEUSER | 55 | 115 |
| □ | 62 | SESSION | 86 | 183 |
| □ | 63 | FILER | 39 | 79 |
| □ | 64 | MENU | 57 | 122 |
| □ | 65 | SECURITY | 83 | 178 |
| □ | 66 | BINDFIX | 14 | 41 |
| □ | 67 | BINDREST | 15 | 43 |
| □ | 68 | ATOTAL | 12 | 39 |
| □ | 69 | PAUDIT | 66 | 140 |
| □ | 70 | TIME | 97 | 204 |
| □ | 71 | SET TIME | 87 | 186 |
| □ | 72 | CONSOLE | 25 | 59 |

# Recommended Learning Sequence


| | Sequence | Description | Module | Page |
|---|---|---|---|---|
| □ | 73 | DOS | 31 | 66 |
| □ | 74 | NAME | 60 | 128 |
| □ | 75 | CONFIG | 24 | 58 |
| □ | 76 | MONITOR | 58 | 125 |
| □ | 77 | OFF | 65 | 139 |
| □ | 78 | DISK | 29 | 63 |
| □ | 79 | BROADCAST | 16 | 44 |
| □ | 80 | SEND (CONSOLE) | 84 | 180 |
| □ | 81 | CLEAR MESSAGE | 22 | 56 |
| □ | 82 | DISABLE LOGIN | 28 | 62 |
| □ | 83 | ENABLE LOGIN | 33 | 69 |
| □ | 84 | CLEAR STATION | 23 | 57 |
| □ | 85 | DOWN | 32 | 67 |
| □ | 86 | QUEUE (CONSOLE 2.1) | 73 | 159 |
| □ | 87 | PRINTER | 70 | 151 |
| □ | 88 | SPOOL | 92 | 193 |
| □ | 89 | QUEUE (CONSOLE) | 74 | 160 |
| □ | 90 | CHANGE QUEUE | 20 | 54 |
| □ | 91 | STOP PRINTER | 94 | 199 |
| □ | 92 | START PRINTER | 93 | 198 |
| □ | 93 | KILL QUEUE | 49 | 99 |
| □ | 94 | KILL PRINTER | 48 | 98 |
| □ | 95 | REROUTE PRINTER | 78 | 168 |
| □ | 96 | REWIND PRINTER | 80 | 172 |
| □ | 97 | FORM CHECK | 41 | 87 |
| □ | 98 | FORM SET | 42 | 88 |
| □ | 99 | MOUNT | 59 | 127 |
| □ | 100 | DISMOUNT | 30 | 65 |
| □ | 101 | ARCHIVE | 11 | 35 |
| □ | 102 | MAIL | 54 | 110 |

To Cynthia, with love. You've made
this, and so much more, possible.

# Module 1

## ABOUT THIS BOOK

### DESCRIPTION

This book describes the implementation and use of a Novell network. Novell NetWare is the best selling high-end network software on the market today and, when combined with the right hardware, can provide a very sophisticated solution to data and resource sharing. The book provides the necessary information to choose the right hardware/software combination, install the network, and become a knowledgeable network administrator or user.

There are numerous hardware options for use with Novell, as well as several versions of NetWare currently being sold—each with different features and limitations. All of these options are covered so that you may put together the ideal network for your specific needs. Software configuration and installation are described in a simple, easy-to-follow format. This allows you to quickly have a running system so that you can begin learning the NetWare commands. The use of each command is described and illustrated with examples that you can type directly at your workstation. Exact syntax of the commands and the resulting screens may vary depending on the NetWare version in use. Commonly made mistakes are pointed out and error messages are explained, relieving you of the frustration many users feel when learning a new software package.

### ORGANIZATION

The book is made up of short modules which are alphabetically arranged for quick reference. There is also a *Recommended Learning Sequence* at the beginning of the book to guide you through the modules in a logical order. The learning sequence also groups the commands by type (public, system, and console) as an aid to each group of readers—installers or technicians, supervisors (network administrators), and beginning users. Like all books in the *Illustrated Series*, the modules are each divided into three main sections: The *Description* section, the *Applications* section, and the *Typical Operation* section.

There are four appendixes. Appendix A is a list of Novell terms and definitions. Appendix B lists commands and their syntax. Appendix C is a chapter of exercises. Appendix D covers Novell's most recent and powerful system, NetWare 386. This appendix gives an overview of the operating system. It also describes the differences between its use and the rest of the NetWare family of products.

Turn to Module 2 to continue the learning sequence.

# Module 2

## AN OVERVIEW OF A NOVELL NETWORK

### COMPONENTS

A Novell local area network (or LAN) consists of a hardware and software combination which allows the sharing of information and resources. While the size, layout, and applications of the Novell LAN vary widely, the basic components are as follows:

- Software Selection
- Network Interface Cards
- One or more Fileservers
- One or more Workstations
- A Cabling System
- Application Software
- Peripheral Devices

Novell publishes several versions of NetWare. They differ in the maximum number of fileservers and users allowed, speed of data transmission, ability to prevent data loss or corruption, and of course, price. While it is possible to upgrade from one version to another, it is usually best to select one that will handle today's and tomorrow's requirements.

Each computer on the network (including fileservers) must contain a network interface card (or NIC). This is the connection through which each computer shares information (via the cabling system) with the others. Novell markets NICs, but so do over a dozen other companies.

The fileservers and workstations can be any of a variety of IBM or compatible personal computers, or computers designed especially for the purpose of being network components. In some Novell configurations, the fileserver doubles as a workstation. The fileserver contains one or more fixed drives; workstations do not require fixed drives, and in some cases even floppy drives are optional.

Most DOS application software will run on a Novell network, but may not take full advantage of the network features. An application designed for network use will usually allow several users to access the same program and data at once, as well as interfacing with shared printers and other peripherals.

## SOFTWARE

Novell NetWare software includes an operating system that runs on network fileservers, software "shells" that run on workstations, and a number of command files and utilities that reside on the fileserver(s). NetWare also comes with installation and configuration programs and diagnostic routines.

The Novell NetWare package contains from 10 to 20 diskettes, as well as a number of manuals. With newer types and versions of NetWare, both 720k (3.5 inch) and 360k (5.25 inch) diskettes are provided. They will include a set of PUBLIC diskettes (usually six), a SYSTEM diskette, a LOGIN diskette, and others (depending on type and version).

**WORKING COPIES** As with any software, you should make duplicates as working copies, and keep the originals safely stored. This is especially important because certain information during the configuration of the software may make permanent changes to files on these diskettes. For years Novell used a copy-protection scheme that required the presence of a serialized "key device" in the fileserver. This has been removed from all versions of NetWare currently being published.

Use the DOS DISKCOPY utility to create a working copy of all NetWare diskettes. Refer to your DOS manual for proper use of DISKCOPY. Simply copying the files on each diskette to pre-formatted blanks will not work, as some of the NetWare programs depend on the volume labels assigned to each diskette.

**SOFTWARE OPTIONS** A number of versions of NetWare have been published. Today there are several available. While NetWare has a version for fileservers based on the 68000 microprocessor (NetWare 68) and a version for the 8088 or "XT-compatible" (NetWare 86), the vast majority of Novell networks being installed today are Advanced NetWare 286. This runs only on 80286- or 80386-based computers, such as the IBM AT or the COMPAQ 386. It is considerably faster than NetWare 86. Workstations on Advanced NetWare 286 networks may be 8088 based.

Today, most versions of NetWare being sold are to some degree "system fault tolerant" (SFT). SFT allows a network to continue functioning in the event of partial failure. This is accomplished through several software features. Duplicate copies of the disk directory and file allocation tables (FATs) are maintained, so that if one should become corrupt, there is a backup. This is a very valuable safety feature—on normal hard disks, a corrupted FAT usually means a complete loss of data. Read-after-write verification detects immediately if the fileserver is attempting to use a section of the hard disk which has gone bad. With a feature called Hot Fix, this section is permanently marked as bad and the data is redirected to an area of the disk reserved for this purpose. These features are built into Advanced NetWare 2.1 and above, as well as ELS (Entry Level Solution) NetWare. With versions below Advanced Netware 2.1, they are only found in systems specified by Novell as SFT Level 1.

An even greater degree of fault tolerance is found in SFT NetWare 2.1, or in the older version—SFT NetWare 2 version 2.0. This includes the ability to have *mirrored disks*. Two identical hard disks are maintained by the system, with all data written to both simultaneously. If one disk fails, a complete backup is still on line. Transaction Tracking System (TTS) is also provided. This tracks multiple updates to data files by your application program, and will cancel the last set of updates if your program is unexpectedly interrupted. As an example, if you are running an accounting package, the entry of an invoice can affect several data files. If the process is interrupted (by a power outage, for instance), the data files will no longer be properly integrated. TTS keeps up with file transactions, and if all updates are not completed, then they are all cancelled.

NetWare is available in both dedicated and nondedicated fileserver versions. A nondedicated fileserver is one that is used simultaneously as a workstation. This can slow the fileserver considerably and, therefore, lower overall network performance. It is best to only use nondedicated fileservers on small networks with relatively light work loads. There is also a risk that a user could accidently lock up, reset, or turn off a fileserver that is being used as a workstation.

The other factor to consider in selecting NetWare is the number of users supported. There is a type of NetWare 86 that only supports a maximum of eight workstations. It is usually marketed by the manufacturers of network interface cards (NICs), who bundle it with their products. ELS NetWare, while loaded with most of the features of the full-blown NetWare 286, is limited to less workstations. ELS NetWare Level I supports four users, and is similar to Advanced NetWare 286 version 2.0. ELS Level II is essentially an eight-user version of Advanced NetWare 286 version 2.15. Most other versions, including NetWare 286, support up to 100 workstations per fileserver.

Select a version of NetWare that will provide you with your current needs and allow for growth. Novell does make available certain upgrades so that if you need the features of a newer NetWare version, you do not have to purchase an entire new system. The new NetWare 386 supports 255 users per fileserver. See Appendix D for an overview of NetWare 386.

## FILESERVERS

The *fileserver* is a mass storage device that is the heart of the Novell network. It contains one or more fixed drives and shares the programs and data they contain with the attached workstations. Various output devices, including printers and plotters, may be attached to a fileserver. These devices are also shared with the workstations. Depending on the type of Novell NetWare in use, a network may contain one or more fileservers.

**COMPUTER TYPE** While a wide variety of DOS computers are available that may be used as fileservers, you must consider the type of NetWare in use before selecting one. Computers using 8088 or 8086 microprocessors are the slowest and ideally are not used as fileservers. These would include the IBM PC XT, IBM PS/2 models 25 and 30, and the COMPAQ DeskPro. 80286- or 80386-based machines provide the speed required for the best fileserver operation. These include the IBM AT and compatibles, IBM PS/2 models 50 and above, and the COMPAQ DeskPro 286 and 386. Novell also markets a line of fileserver computers.

NetWare 86 is designed for use on an 8088/8086-based machine, though it is more typically used with an 80286- or even 80386-based machine for increased speed. NetWare 286 runs only on 80286- or 80386-based machines. It is designed to take full advantage of the 80286 and therefore is considerably faster than NetWare 86. ELS NetWare will run only on certain makes of machines. This is because it requires a very high degree of IBM BIOS compatibility. There are several machines which may be used, but be sure to check with the manufacturer or your dealer to verify compatibility.

Each fileserver must contain a network interface card (NIC). This communicates through the cable system to the NICs in each workstation. With some types of NetWare the fileserver must also contain a keycard, which is included in the NetWare package. As the fileserver will not function without the keycard, this prevents the unauthorized use of the NetWare software on more than one network.

**HARD DRIVES** The fileserver must contain at least one hard drive. This contains the NetWare system files and utilities as well as the applications software and data. You prepare the hard drive with Novell's own format routine (as opposed to DOS) as part of the installation.

Most brands of hard drives that are compatible with your fileserver will work. If you are using an 80286- or 80386-based machine, it is important to select drives that are of a "standard type" for the brand of computer you have chosen. The drive type is determined by its number of read/write heads, the number of cylinders, and other technical specifications. Different manufacturers of computers consider various drive types standard. Nonstandard drives are often used by formatting them with special utilities. Because Novell uses its own format, these utilities may not work. There are also a number of disk subsystems (hard drives mounted in a chassis outside of the fileserver) that are compatible with NetWare. The speed of the drive should also be considered. With a number of users relying on information from a drive at once, a slow drive can lower the overall system performance.

**FILESERVER RAM** The minimum amount of memory (or RAM) depends on both the type of NetWare in use and the size of your hard drive(s). NetWare 86 fileservers should have 640K RAM. NetWare 286 and ELS NetWare 286 can access extended memory. Nondedicated fileservers require memory for both fileserver and workstation applications, thus 640K base memory with 1 megabyte or more extended memory is recommended. Dedicated NetWare 286 may get by with as little as 640K. Novell uses a portion of RAM for hashing and (if configured to) caching of hard drives. Put simply, this means that commonly used information from the drives is kept in RAM for quick access and greatly improved system speed. The larger the drive(s), the more RAM that is needed for this task. An 80-megabyte total hard drive storage can be accomodated with the preceding configurations. Larger drives may need more.

**UPS** An uninterruptible power supply (UPS) is strongly recommended for fileservers. This provides continuous power to the system in the event of a power outage. Because of the hashing and caching process described above, the system should be properly shut down to prevent loss or corruption of data. The UPS allows the operator time to do this. SFT NetWare provides a feature called "UPS monitoring." When used with a UPS that is designed to support this feature, the fileserver is alerted if the battery is almost drained (during prolonged power outages). The fileserver then proceeds to bring down the network in a safe manner.

## WORKSTATIONS

Workstations are the individual computers through which you access the network. Each workstation is assigned a unique address (via settings on its network interface card). To the user, however, NetWare seems to make no distinction between workstations. In other words, the ability to access various resources on the network is determined by who is using the system, not which workstation they are using.

**COMPUTER TYPES** Workstations can be almost any IBM, COMPAQ, AT&T, or compatible DOS computer. They must have one expansion slot available for the NIC. There are a few machines that may not function properly on a Novell network. This is especially true of some of the very early compatibles. Check with the manufacturer or your dealer to be sure.

**HARD DRIVES** The drives of the fileserver are made available to each workstation in a fairly transparent way. This means that accessing them is very similar to accessing drives on a stand-alone computer. A "local" hard drive can be used in a workstation, but is not needed. At least one floppy drive is needed to allow DOS and the NetWare shell (software that communicates with the network) to be loaded. This need is eliminated with the use of certain NICs that contain a "Boot ROM" which allows this software to be loaded directly off the fileserver.

**WORKSTATION RAM** The NetWare shell stays in memory and may require up to 64K of workstation RAM. Therefore, each workstation should have at least 64K in addition to the memory needed for DOS and user applications. Generally it is ideal to provide each workstation with 640K total RAM.

## NETWORK INTERFACE CARDS

Network fileservers and workstations communicate with each other through network interface cards (NICs). Each computer on the network must contain a NIC. The NIC occupies one expansion slot in the computer and provides an external connection to which the network cable is attached. There are several cabling schemes available, but the network cable in some way connects all the computers on the network.

Over a dozen manufacturers provide NICs that are Novell compatible. At the time of installation, you specify which NIC you will be using; NetWare configures itself to communicate through the particular card you select. Within one network, all NICs must be of the same type, but not necessarily the same manufacturer. There are several standards that have been established, and for each standard there may be multiple companies that make their own version. Two or more networks using different types or standards of NICs may be interconnected via a process called *bridging*. A bridge is essentially one fileserver (or in some cases workstation) that has two or more NICs, each cabled to a different network.

There are a number of specifications that differentiate the various NICs available for Novell networking. The main ones to consider are discussed in the following sections.

**TYPE OF CABLING** Cabling is often the first consideration in selecting the type of network hardware you will use. Each type of NIC has particular cable requirements. Different cable types include broad and base band (coaxial), twisted pair (same as telephone wiring), multi-conductor (usually 9 wire), and even fiber optic. Some NICs may allow the use of more than one type of cable; however, the cable you choose to use must be the same throughout the network.

**SPEED OF TRANSMISSION** The speed at which data is transmitted over the network is determined by the NIC. It is measured in bits per second. A *bit* is the smallest unit of data, represented by a 1 or 0. Cards are rated in kilobits (thousand bits) or megabits (million bits) per second. Depending on the NIC you select, your network may communicate at anywhere from 500 kilobits/second (or .5 megabits) to 20 megabits/second, and above!

**METHOD OF COLLISION CONTROL** In a network environment workstations and fileservers communicate with each other over a system of cabling. Because several computers may need to access the network simultaneously, there must be some way to control traffic.

One such method is called token passing. A *token* is a special string of data that is sent over the network, from one computer to the next. Whichever computer has the token may "broadcast" data or data requests over the network. Each computer must wait its turn to broadcast, thus collisions of data cannot occur. This whole process happens very quickly, so to the user it appears that all computers are communicating at once. ARCnet and Token-Ring are two NIC standards that use this method.

Another popular method is to allow all computers to broadcast as needed. The network monitors this process and is able to detect data collisions. When one occurs, all NICs back up a step and begin transmitting their last data over again. This method is very fast in most networks; however, in very large networks the number of collisions can increase exponentially and erode overall performance. An example of this method, known as "carrier sense multiple access collision detection and avoidance," (CSMA/CD) is the Ethernet NIC.

**NETWORK DISTANCE** In choosing a NIC and cabling scheme, bear in mind the total area which the network will cover. Each manufacturer publishes distance specifications for their products. With some NICs, you may have the option of using different types of cables, and/or signal boosters, to attain maximum distances. There are also products available to allow networks to be bridged across considerable distances, using fiber optics, microwave, or dedicated phone lines.

**BUFFER SIZE** NICs have memory on them to serve as a *buffer* between the card and the network. This allows the NIC to transmit or receive data while the computer attends to other tasks. The larger the buffer a NIC has, the faster the overall operation can be.

**DATA BUS SIZE** Most NICs are designed to fit in the 8-bit data bus slot of IBM PC XTs and compatibles. These cards will also work in 286/386 level machines, but only as 8-bit cards. (This means the NIC communicates with the computer 8 bits at a time.) Some manufacturers have 16-bit versions of their cards available. These work only in 286/386 computers but speed overall network access considerably. Even if you do not use 16-bit NICs in workstations, you should consider using them in fileservers.

## OVERALL SPEED

The performance of a NIC depends upon the speed of transmission, the way it handles collisions, the amount of buffer memory on board, and the size of the data bus. The speed of the network can depend upon a number of factors, including speed of fileserver(s), speed of workstation(s), speed of shared hard disk(s), number of users, and speed of NICs. Therefore, it is not always advisable to buy very expensive, state-of-the-art NICs if the rest of the network is not fast enough to take full advantage of them. At the same time, don't negate the power of high-speed workstations by using excessively slow NICs.

Complete technical specifications on various NICs are available from the manufacturers or your computer dealer.

Turn to Module 3 to continue the learning sequence.

# Module 3

## HARDWARE INSTALLATION

After selecting the appropriate products for your Novell network, it is time to install and configure the hardware components. This includes cabling, network interface cards, fileservers, and workstations. The installation of hard drives and interface cards and the running and connecting of network cable can be a difficult job. There are numerous potential pitfalls and the job is best left to professional network installers. However, if you want to undertake this yourself, keep these tips in mind:

- The cable is the lifeline of your network. When running it, be sure that it is not at risk of being damaged or worn. This is especially important with certain types of network interface cards (NICs), such as Ethernet, because a broken cable can shut down the entire network.
- Stick to the exact cable specified by the manufacturer of the NICs you are using. Using the wrong cable can prevent the network from operating at all or, worse yet, cause intermittent problems that may be very difficult to trace back to the cable.
- Take extra care when fastening the connectors on the cable. A sloppy connection can cause severe problems down the road.
- Read carefully the installation instructions for the NICs before attempting to install them. Wrong switch or jumper settings can affect one workstation, or the entire network.
- If the NICs you are using have selectable node address settings (such as ARCnet), set the addresses on all cards before installing any of them. Make a record of which cards have which address, so that when expanding in the future, you will know which addresses are still available.
- Remember that static discharge when touching computer components can cause costly damage.

- Use great care in handling hard drives. Even a slight jolt to the drive can cause permanent damage.
- When expanding RAM memory, be sure to use chips that are rated at sufficient speed for the computer you are using. Different manufacturers require different types of RAM.

Turn to Module 4 to continue the learning sequence.

# Module 4
## COMPSURF

### DESCRIPTION

The COMPSURF utility formats and performs extensive tests on the fileserver drive(s). These tests assure the drive's suitability for the network and also locate and mark any bad areas. The use hard drives receive on networks is much more demanding than in most single-user applications and, therefore, the testing is more comprehensive. Depending on the size of the drive, COMPSURF can take anywhere from 4 to more than 16 hours. It is possible that COMPSURF will reject a drive that a standard DOS format would accept as usable. Fortunately, when this occurs it is usually early in the testing procedure. Some manufacturers (including Novell) ship drives that have already undergone COMPSURF. This should be stated in the documentation accompanying the drive.

**INITIAL INSTALLATION** With ELS NetWare Level I, COMPSURF is located on the START diskette and is invoked by the START batch file (see Module 7). ELS Level II has a menu-driven utility called ELSGEN that generates and invokes COMPSURF, as well as other aspects of NetWare installation. With NetWare 286 versions 2.1 and above, a similar utility called NETGEN (see Module 5) serves the same purpose. With older versions of NetWare, it is found on the INSTALL diskette and must be manually run before proceeding to the INSTALL procedure. The utility destroys existing data and should be used with care.

**ADDING ADDITIONAL DRIVES** With all types of NetWare, COMPSURF can be manually run to prepare hard drives that are being added to an existing fileserver. Be careful to select the correct drive for formatting.

### TYPICAL OPERATION

In this activity, you format and perform extensive tests on your hard drive before installing Novell NetWare. Because COMPSURF will destroy all data on the drive, it is important to have a complete understanding of the particular version of COMPSURF you are using. Refer to the NetWare installation manual for more details. Start COMPSURF according to the manual's instructions.

The screen will resemble:

```
DISK FORMATTER and COMPREHENSIVE SURFACE
ANALYSIS PROGRAM (C) Copyright Novell Inc. 1983,
1984, 1985, 1986

Version: AN286 2.0 Date: 12 Nov 1988

**** WARNING ****

THIS PROGRAM COMPLETELY ERASES ALL DATA ON THE DISK

Enter today's date:
```

1. Using the MM/DD/YY format, type today's date and press **Enter**. The screen now lists all present hard drives. If the list is incorrect, your drives may be improperly installed. If you have one drive installed, the screen should resemble the following:

```
The following disk drive(s) are attached to
this PC:

1. IBM Hard Disk "C" type 08

Select the drive to be tested.
```

**CAUTION**

The drive you select is not only tested, but first formatted, destroying any data on it.

2. Type the appropriate drive number; in this case, with only one drive present you would type **1**. Press **Enter**. The screen now shows:

```
Enter the interleave (1-16)
```

The interleave value determines how data is stored on the drive. The lower the number, the faster the data is written and retrieved. If, however, you use an interleave too low, your system may not be able to keep up, resulting in greatly impaired speed. Most systems perform best with a value of 2.

3. Type **2** and press **Enter**. Now the screen shows:

```
Enter the number of times to repeat the
regular surface analysis (0-3):
```

It is the surface analysis that takes the majority of the time spent running COMPSURF. To assure greatest dependability, it is recommended that you select three repetitions of this process. Very roughly speaking, the analysis takes about 30 minutes per 10 megabytes of drive space for each repetition. Therefore, selecting three repetitions with an 80-megabyte drive may take up to 12 hours or more.

4. Type **3** and press **Enter**. The screen now asks:

```
Read the "bad block" list from the disk?
(y/n)
```

5. Type **N** and press **Enter** as COMPSURF often cannot read any existing table of defective drive areas (or bad blocks), and COMPSURF does an extensive job of finding all bad blocks. The screen now verifies the information you have entered. An example follows:

```
              Date:    1/12/89
        Disk Model:    IBM Hard DISK "C"
                       type 08
  Controller type:     IBM

The disk will be FORMATTED!
The interleave = 2
The "surface" test will be repeated 3 time(s).
The existing bad block list will not be retained.

Are these entries correct? (y/n)
```

6. Type **N** to change any of the listed information or type **Y** to proceed with the format/testing.

7. Press **Enter**. For the next several hours, COMPSURF displays various information on the screen as it formats the drive, and performs sequential read/write tests. Next a random seek test begins. This runs until you interrupt it. Allow it to run an additional two to six hours, then proceed to step 8.
8. Type **S** and press **Enter**. COMPSURF responds with:

```
Do you really want to terminate the test?
```

9. Type **YY** and press **Enter**. COMPSURF asks:

```
Would you like to print the error report?
(yy/nn)
```

10. If you wish to maintain a list of all bad blocks which COMPSURF has marked, type **YY** and press **Enter**. This report could prove useful in the event that the bad block table on your drive is ever deleted. Otherwise type **NN** and press **Enter**. COMPSURF is now complete.
11. Turn to Module 5 to continue the learning sequence.

# Module 5

## NET$OS

### DESCRIPTION

The heart of Novell NetWare's operating system is a program named NET$OS. It is an executable (.EXE) file located on the fileserver. NET$OS controls network communication, servicing requests from all attached workstations for disk I/O, network printer access, and messaging. While many of the public and console commands are the same in all versions of NetWare, NET$OS differs with each version. On dedicated fileservers (ones which cannot be used as workstations) NET$OS is located on the first network hard drive, and is loaded automatically upon booting the computer. DOS is not present in the operation of dedicated fileservers. Nondedicated fileservers usually load NET$OS from a diskette. This "fileserver boot diskette" loads DOS, then NET$OS (often called from the AUTOEXEC.BAT file). Once NET$OS is running (as a "background" operation) the fileserver returns to DOS and is useable as an extra workstation.

Under Advanced or SFT NetWare 286 and ELS NetWare Level II, the NET$OS program must be generated at the time of network installation. The program exists on the Novell diskettes in a nonexecutable form. Using the generation program (called GENOS with NetWare version 2.0, and NETGEN with 2.1 and above), you provide information concerning your fileserver configuration. This information is used in creating the executable form of NET$OS. Finally, NET$OS is installed on the fileserver hard drive by the INSTALL program of version 2.0 or the NETGEN program of version 2.1 and above.

ELS NetWare Level II uses ELSGEN to create NET$OS. ELS NetWare Level I comes with NET$OS already generated. You are provided with a separate executable copy for each of the available network interface cards that ELS supports. The appropriate NET$OS is simply copied onto the fileserver boot diskette.

## TYPICAL OPERATION

NET$OS and the related generation programs change considerably with each version of NetWare. For details on proper generation and installation of NET$OS, refer to your NetWare installation manual.

Turn to Module 6 to continue the learning sequence.

# Module 6

## INSTALL

### DESCRIPTION

The INSTALL utility is valid only under Advanced NetWare versions 2.0 and below. Versions 2.1 and above use a considerably more sophisticated windowing utility called NETGEN. ELS NetWare Level II uses a utility called ELSGEN. These utilities have numerous available options and change frequently; therefore, refer to the Novell installation manual for details on the use of INSTALL for maintaining existing networks under versions 2.0 and below. INSTALL sets up a drive for NetWare and installs the appropriate NetWare programs on it. INSTALL is also used to configure the various system parameters, change certain system information, and assign network printers. This utility should be used with considerable care, as it can destroy existing data on fileserver network drive(s).

### APPLICATIONS

INSTALL is used as part of the initial network installation after COMPSURF has formatted and tested the drive(s) (see Module 4). For ELS NetWare Level I INSTALL is invoked by the START routine (see Module 7). For other types of NetWare, it is usually run in an automated mode which uses default information to set up the fileserver. With all types of NetWare, it also allows manual, step-by-step operation for custom or unique installations. It is through this manual mode that you can change the setup information if it ever becomes necessary in the future.

### TYPICAL OPERATION

**NOTE**

If you have ELS NetWare Level I and you are performing your initial installation, skip to Module 7, START.

In this operation, you begin with the fileserver turned off. If INSTALL is being run on a fileserver with previously INSTALLED drive(s), be sure to properly bring the system down.

1. Place a bootable DOS diskette in drive A and turn the system on. When DOS is loaded remove the diskette from drive A.
2. Place the INSTALL diskette in drive A. Type **INSTALL** at the A> prompt and press **Enter**. Your screen should resemble the following:

```
NetWare   Installation   Utility   V2.00   (c)
Copyright 1983, 1985 by Novell, Inc.

This  utility is used to initialize a hard disk
for use by the NetWare network.  Setting  up  a
disk   involves   allocating  a  partition  for
NetWare  on  the  IBM  hard  disk.   Once   the
partition  has  been  allocated,  it is divided
into one or more volumes.  The volumes are then
initialized  with the directory structures used
by NetWare.

This  utility   is   designed   so   that   the
initialization    process     is    relatively
straightforward.  If you are not certain if you
should  be  using this utility,  type an "H" to
get additional help;  otherwise, type any other
character to proceed.  (Type a Ctrl-C to  abort
this program.)
```

If the terminology confuses you, don't worry. Each step will be carefully explained.

3. Press any key (except H) to continue; the screen responds with:

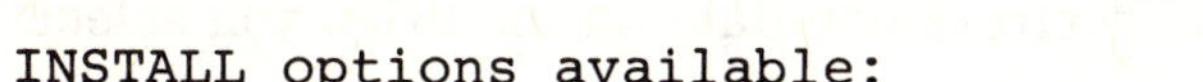

```
INSTALL options available:

1.  Initially  set up a disk for NetWare.  --->
Note: Options 2-9 are normally
              used only to work with
              existing NetWare systems and
              usually are not needed when
              you bring up a new system.
2.    Edit or install a partition table.
3.    Initialize NetWare volume directory
      areas.
4.    Install the cold boot loaders.
5.    Install the system and public files.
6.    Edit miscellaneous system parameters.
7.    Edit or install the spooled printer list.
8.    Edit NetWare volume directory sizes and
      options.
9.    Remove NetWare physical disks.
10.   Exit INSTALL.

Enter the option desired: _
```

For first time installations, or when adding a new drive to the fileserver, continue with OPTION 1. For other requirements, read the descriptions of the other options.

## OPTION 1

1. Type **1** and press **Enter** to select option 1. (If you require custom information assigned in options 6 through 8, you may do so after running option 1.) The screen reads:

```
Set Up a Disk for NetWare.

You can specify the installation parameters, or
you can use a pre-defined set of parameters. If
you choose the default parameters, you can
change most of them later without losing your
existing files.

Do you want to use the default installation
parameters (y/n): _
```

2. To proceed with the standard complete installation process, type **Y** and press **Enter**.

You are now asked to select the drive to be initialized. As with COMPSURF, be careful, as this process destroys any data on the drive you select.

3. Type the DOS letter of the drive and press **Enter**. From here the INSTALL routine partitions the selected drive as one NetWare volume, then initializes the volume. Your next input is prompted with a screen similar to this:

```
Volume names may not contain spaces, colons,
asterisks, question marks, slashes, or
backslashes. The first character may not be a
period.

Enter the new volume name (2 to 15
characters):
```

4. If this is the first volume on this fileserver, the default name "SYS" is automatically used. In this case, we are naming the volume "VOL1." Type **VOL1** and press **Enter**. Next you are prompted, one by one, to place various diskettes in drive A. INSTALL loads from these diskettes all necessary NetWare utilities into the new volume.

When this process is complete, the main INSTALL menu is displayed again.

5. If you need to edit the default information which was just installed, type the number of the option (described as follows) and press **Enter**. Otherwise, type **10** and press **Enter** to exit INSTALL.
6. To continue the learning sequence, turn to Module 7.

**OPTION 2** The default partition table allocates the entire drive to one partition. There is generally no reason to edit this. If you do, remember that changing the partition destroys all data on that drive.

**OPTION 3** As there is only one way to initialize volume directory areas (the default), there should be no reason to use this option manually. If, however, you should remove a drive from the network (option 9) and later wish to reinstall it without losing your data, you must use this utility.

**OPTION 4** The cold boot loaders are system files needed to boot a fileserver without the use of DOS. These are installed by option 1; there is no need to do it again.

**OPTION 5** This option simply copies the NetWare utility files into the appropriate directories. Once again, option 1 does this for you.

**OPTION 6** This allows you to alter three parameters. You will be asked if you wish to change each of them. The first, the cache block size, affects the caching and therefore the speed of the fileserver. The second, maximum number of files open at once, may need to be changed as a network grows or if software applications are added which use unusually large numbers of open files. With these first two parameters, the larger the value given, the more total memory (RAM) that is used. Too large a value may cause warnings on fileserver boot-up and may prevent caching of the hard drive(s). The final parameter is the fileserver name. Should you ever have a reason to change it, that may be accomplished here.

**OPTION 7** This is where you define what printers are attached to which filesever ports and whether they are serial or parallel. For serial printers, you also define baud rate, parity, etc. Refer to your printer's user manual for this information. Each printer is given a network number, beginning with 0. Record this information, as it is used to direct printouts from workstations to the correct network printer.

**OPTION 8** Use this option to change the volume name, volume flag, or volume directory size. Generally the defaults are not changed. If you change the volume flag from "cached" to "not cached," the network's speed will be considerably slowed.

**OPTION 9** To physically remove a drive from your fileserver, select this option. The system drive (drive 0) cannot be removed. Always back up any needed data from a drive before removing it.

**OPTION 10** When you are finished with INSTALL, type 10 and press Enter. The fileserver reboots.

To continue the learning sequence, turn to Module 7.

# Module 7
## START

### DESCRIPTION

ELS NetWare Level I has simplified the software installation process by providing a batch file called START.BAT. This is located on a diskette labeled START which is not provided with other types of NetWare. If you are using any other version of NetWare, skip this module.

### APPLICATIONS

The START utility automatically invokes COMPSURF (see Module 4) and INSTALL (Module 6). It is only used when setting up the original (or system) drive. Additional drives should be prepared by manually invoking COMPSURF and INSTALL, being careful not to overwrite existing drive(s).

### TYPICAL OPERATION

In this activity, you install your ELS NetWare version of software.

1. Place a bootable DOS diskette in the fileserver drive A and turn the system on. With the system booted, remove the DOS diskette and insert the NetWare diskette labeled START.
2. At the A> prompt, type **START** and press **Enter**.

**NOTE**

If you do not have at least 512K extended memory, the START utility quits and you are returned to a DOS prompt.

```
WARNING: This procedure will destroy all data
on drive C:! If you haven't already done so,
make a backup copy of all files on your hard
disk.

Do you want to continue? (y/n)
```

3. As this should be your initial installation, there should be no data on drive C. Assuming this is true, type **Y** and press **Enter**.

You are prompted for the DOS diskette again and then asked to return the START diskette to drive A. Now the START utility formats and tests the drive. Although the screen shows the amount of time this process should take, it is not always accurate. Allow the system as much time as needed to finish this stage of the installation. The amount of time will vary according to the size of your drive; the screen will report an approximation. When this is complete the screen prompts:

```
The test of your hard disk was successful,
Strike a key when ready...
```

4. Press any key. START partitions and initializes the drive. The screen says:

```
Preparing the drive and creating the NetWare
Volume.
```

followed by:

```
Copying NetWare SYSTEM and PUBLIC files and
utilities.
```

5. When prompted, place the various NetWare diskettes, one by one, in drive A. START loads from these all necessary NetWare utilities into the new volume. When finished, the screen reads:

```
System files successfully installed.
Strike a key when ready...
```

6. Press any key. Insert the START disk when you are prompted:

```
Insert disk START in any drive.
Strike a key when ready...
```

At this point the fileserver software installation is complete.

7. Turn to Module 8 to continue the learning sequence.

# Module 8

## WORKSTATION SHELLS (ANET AND NET)

### DESCRIPTION

The only part of NetWare that must reside on workstations is a program called the "workstation shell." When a workstation is booted with DOS, the appropriate shell program must be loaded before you can access the network (see Booting the System, Module 10). The shell controls workstation communication (through the network interface card, or NIC) with the network. Like NET$OS (Module 5), the workstation shells may differ with each version of NetWare.

Under Advanced NetWare 286 version 2.0, the shell must be generated using the GENSH program. NetWare 2.1 and above provides the shell already generated; however, a program called SHGEN is still used to generate a custom interface for the shell. Either way, as a part of the GENSH process, you provide configuration information about your workstations. This includes the type of NIC in use and the address and interrupt values that were set on the NIC at the time of installation. Information about these settings is found in the documentation that is provided with the NICs. Because SHGEN and GENSH write to the diskettes used during the shell generation process, it is important to use copies of the original diskettes (see Module 2). Version 2.0 creates two shells—ANET2.COM and ANET3.COM. Use ANET2.COM for workstations running DOS 2.x, and ANET3.COM for DOS3.x. (NetWare will not run under DOS 1.x.) It is not necessary for all workstations on the network to run the same version of DOS, although it tends to reduce confusion. NetWare versions 2.1 and above (including ELS Level II) use three shells, NET2.COM, NET3.COM, and NET4.COM, along with the interface file called IPX.COM. IPX.COM is loaded prior to NETx.COM.

ELS NetWare Level I has a set of ready-to-use workstation shells called ANETx.COM. There is a separate shell diskette for each NIC type.

## TYPICAL OPERATION

Workstation shells and the related generation programs change considerably with each version of NetWare. For details on proper generation and installation of these shells, refer to your NetWare installation manual.

Turn to Module 9 to continue the learning sequence.

# Module 9

## TROUBLESHOOTING

Installing a network seldom goes without the need for some degree of troubleshooting. While NetWare is an excellent (and fairly straightforward) product, the network as a whole brings together many different components, often from several different manufacturers. If your network doesn't work properly the first time you try to boot it, don't worry! The following guide should help you find and resolve the problem(s).

### COMMON PROBLEMS

The following are some of the most common problems encountered when booting a NetWare network. Other problems may require support from Novell, the hardware manufacturer, or a networking professional.

| *Problem* | *Solution* |
|---|---|
| *FILESERVER* | |
| The fileserver hard drive will not format (COMPSURF, Module 4). | • Check the drive for proper cabling and jumper settings. This information varies with each drive. Details should be available in the installation manual, from your dealer, or from the manufacturer.<br>• With 286 or 386 fileservers, make sure that the correct drive type has been selected through the setup program that came with the computer.<br>• Try a different hard drive controller. A controller may seem to work with DOS, and yet fail NetWare's rigorous format and drive analysis.<br>• The hard drive may be defective. Bear in mind that a drive may format under DOS, but not be acceptable for NetWare. COMPSURF is particularly sensitive to problems with track 0 on a drive. |
| After successfully installing NetWare, the fileserver will not boot. This is often accompanied by the error message "ABEND." | • Check the NIC for proper installation, and make sure the keycard is installed (not applicable to versions of NetWare that are not copy-protected). |

| Problem | Solution |
| --- | --- |
| | • Test the memory (RAM) of the fileserver. A defective chip will often show up during fileserver boot.<br>• Try a different hard drive controller. A controller may seem to work with DOS, and may even work through the format and installation, and yet not allow the fileserver to boot.<br>• Make sure your fileserver is compatible with NetWare. This is particularly important with ELS NetWare, which is not compatible with the ROM BIOS of some computers.<br>• If the fileserver is nondedicated (such as some of those running ELS NetWare), make sure that a good, bootable diskette is in drive A.<br>• Certain types of network interface cards (such as Ethernet) will not allow the fileserver to boot if the cable is not properly run. Check for bad connections and, if used, proper installation of terminating connectors. |
| Fileserver indicates that there is not enough memory to cache a directory or a drive. | • Caching is the process of using RAM memory to speed hard drive access. A fileserver will run without caching, but will probably perform too slowly. If this is the case, expand the RAM on the fileserver. With nondedicated ELS NetWare, remember that the fileserver is doubling as a workstation and requires sufficient memory for both tasks. |
| *WORKSTATION* | |
| Upon running the workstation shell, you get the message "A Fileserver Could Not Be Found," or the system locks up. | • Check the network interface card (NIC) for proper installation, including address and interrupt settings.<br>• Try a different NIC. Yours may be defective.<br>• Check the cable for good connections. Take note of whether or not other workstations can boot onto the network. This will indicate a potential cable problem is at the workstation or the fileserver.<br>• Check the NIC node setting to be sure that it is not the same as another NIC on the network. With some types of NICs (such as Ethernet), each card is shipped with a permanant, unique node address. |

Turn to Module 10 to continue the learning sequence.

# Module 10
## BOOTING THE SYSTEM

### DESCRIPTION

Turning on a fully installed network and bringing it on-line is a process referred to as *booting the system*. Before doing this, you should complete Modules 1 through 9. The fileserver(s) must be booted prior to any workstations being turned on. Many network administrators choose to leave the fileserver always booted and available to the network. Others choose to bring down the fileserver each night and reboot it each morning. Workstations are turned on and booted onto the network each day, though they should only be logged in to the network (see Module 51) when in use.

Booting fileservers essentially consists of turning on the computer and loading the NET$OS program. Dedicated fileservers (ones that do not double as workstations) have NET$OS on their first hard drive. The computer is turned on with the floppy drive open, and a system program called the "cold boot loader" loads and starts NET$OS. Nondedicated fileservers load NET$OS from a diskette (referred to as the "fileserver boot diskette"). The computer is turned on, with the boot diskette in drive A. DOS loads from the diskette, then an AUTOEXEC.BAT file loads NET$OS. Finally, with NET$OS running as a background task, the fileserver returns to a DOS prompt, ready to use as a workstation. Use CONSOLE and DOS (Modules 25 and 31) to toggle between the fileserver and workstation modes.

Booting workstations requires turning on the computer, booting DOS, and loading the appropriate workstation shell. DOS may be booted from a hard drive or from floppy drive A. The shell must be configured for the network interface card in use. For a more detailed explanation of the workstation shell, see Module 8. Once the shell (IPX.COM and NETx.COM or ANETx.COM) is running, the first network drive will be available. On workstations running DOS 3.x this will usually be drive F. From this drive, you can log in to the network.

An increasingly popular network computer is the *diskless* workstation. This is a computer with memory, microprocessor, screen, and keyboard, but without hard or floppy drives. The built-in network interface card contains a permanent memory chip (called the *boot ROM*) that contains the workstation shell. To boot the diskless workstation, simply turn it on. DOS is loaded from the fileserver over the network.

Bringing a workstation down simply requires logging out (Module 53) and turning off the computer. At the fileserver, use DOWN (Module 32) to close any open files and the disk cache, and turn off the computer. It is important to make sure that all users have logged out (or at least exited any application) before using DOWN, and it is vital that you run DOWN before powering off or resetting the fileserver.

## TYPICAL OPERATION

In this activity, you boot the network starting with the fileserver. With dedicated fileservers begin with drive A open; with nondedicated fileservers place the boot diskette in drive A.

1. Turn on the fileserver. The fileserver screen will show various information about the drive(s) that are being mounted and cached, the copyright message, and the date and time. When the fileserver is fully booted, the screen displays the console prompt, a colon. Now, the workstations can be booted.
2. Turn on the workstation and boot DOS. If the workstation has a hard drive, it probably contains DOS. Floppy drive systems will need a bootable DOS diskette in drive A. Diskless workstations will load DOS from the fileserver. If you are not using a diskless workstation, execute the workstation shell (see Module 8). Floppy drive machines will contain the shell on the bootable DOS diskette. On hard drive machines, change to the directory containing the shell. When you see the DOS prompt, continue to step 3.
3. For NetWare 2.1 and above, or for ELS NetWare Level II, type **IPX** and press **Enter**. The screen will display information concerning the NIC configuration. Then type **NET2**, **NET3**, or **NET4** (depending on your DOS version; DOS 3.x, for instance, uses NET3) and press **Enter**. For NetWare 2.0 and below, or for ELS NetWare Level I, type **ANET3** or **ANET2**, and press **Enter**. The screen will resemble the following:

```
A>NET3
Advanced NetWare V2.01-3 Workstation Shell for PC DOS V3.x
Copyright (c) by Novell, Inc. 1983, 1987

LAN Option: Novell RX-Net

Attached to server MAIN
Thursday, January 5, 1989    3:55:07 pm

A>
```

If it does not, refer to Troubleshooting, Module 9.

Next, you create the necessary files and directories needed to continue the learning sequence. A basic knowledge of DOS is helpful for these steps. First you must log in to your fileserver.

4. Type **F:** and press **Enter**.
5. Type **LOGIN SUPERVISOR** and press **Enter**. If this is not a new network you will have to be assigned a user name by your network supervisor.
6. Type **MD\INN** and press **Enter**.
7. Type **CD\INN** and press **Enter**.
8. Type **COPY CON TEST.TXT** and press **Enter**. The cursor returns to the left edge of the screen.
9. Type **THIS IS A TEST** and press **Enter**. The cursor again returns to the edge.
10. Type **Ctrl-Z** and press **Enter**.
11. Repeat steps 7-9 using the following filenames. For example, the next file you need to create is REPORT.TXT. Insert REPORT.TXT where you typed TEST.TXT in step 7.

    REPORT.TXT
    SALES.LET
    TEST.PRN
    321.EXE
12. Type **COPY CON START.BAT** and press **Enter**.
13. Type **DIR** and press **Enter**. This will cause a directory listing to be displayed each time this batch file is used.
14. Type **Ctrl-Z** and press **Enter**.
15. Repeat steps 10-12 using the filename GO.BAT.

Next, you create two users that are needed throughout the learning sequence.

16. Type **SYSCON** and press **Enter**.
17. Press **Down Arrow** to highlight "User Information" and press **Enter**.
18. Press **Insert**.
19. Type **FRED** and press **Enter**.
20. Press **Enter**.
21. Press **Down Arrow** to highlight "Security Equivalences" and press **Enter**.
22. Press **Down Arrow** to highlight "SUPERVISOR" and press **Enter**.
23. Press **Esc**.
24. Press **Up Arrow** to highlight "Password" and press **Enter**.
25. Type **SUNSHINE** and press **Enter**.
26. Press **Esc**.
27. Repeat steps 17-26 using the username BOB.
28. Press **Esc** twice and press **Enter** to exit SYSCON.
29. Turn to Module 51 to continue the learning sequence.

# Module 11

## ARCHIVE

### DESCRIPTION

NetWare provides utilities for archiving (or backing up) network files. LARCHIVE and LRESTORE archive and restore files to local (workstation) drives. NARCHIVE and NRESTORE use network drives to store the archived files. These utilities are used on networks in place of the DOS commands BACKUP and RESTORE.

LARCHIVE and NARCHIVE work basically the same. The command can be issued by itself, or followed by the drive, volume, directory command, or filename(s) you wish to archive. Unlike the DOS BACKUP command, Novell's ARCHIVE is *interactive*. That is, it asks a series of questions to determine which files will be included (or excluded) in the backup and where they will be sent.

### APPLICATIONS

Periodic archiving of files is vital. Even the best of networks and computers can suddenly lose part or all of your data at any time. There is no way to predict when a drive failure may occur. Building fires and computer theft also pose threats to your data. Archiving is especially important with networks, because many users' data may be stored in one place.

For complete system backups of the fileserver hard drive it is probably best to use a streaming tape backup system. This will quickly and easily transfer network data to small tape cartridges. Be sure to use a tape system that comes with NetWare compatible software.

### TYPICAL OPERATION

In this activity, you archive the contents of the directory SYS:INN to your local drive A. Begin at the DOS prompt of a logged in workstation.

1. Type **LARCHIVE SYS:INN** and press **Enter**. The screen shows:

```
F:\>LARCHIVE SYS:INN
Advanced NetWare LARCHIVE V1.12 -- Archive to Local Disks
Copyrights (C) 1984, 1985, 1986 Novell, Inc. All Rights
Reserved.

Enter the letter of the LOCAL disk drive on which to archive
files:
```

2. Type **A** and press **Enter**. You are asked "Do you want to print a log report of this session? (Y/N) N."

It is best to always print this report. However, since this is just for practice, you can skip it.

3. Type **N** and press **Enter**. Next you are asked "Do you want to save directory rights and trustee lists? (Y/N) N."
4. Type **N** and press **Enter**. The next question is "Do you want to archive the system's user and group definitions? (Y/N) N."
5. Type **N** and press **Enter**. Now you see:

```
Select specific directories to be backed up? (Y/N)
(N = Back up all directories) N
```

If you had not specified the directory to archive, you would now be asked, one at a time, which directories to include. Instead, select all directories; only the one specified will be archived.

6. Type **N** and press **Enter**. The next selection is:

```
Select the backup mode for this directory from the following:
1) Back up ALL qualified files in each directory
2) Back up ONLY qualified files that have been modified since
   last backup
3) Choose specific files to be backed up

Select Option: (1-3)
```

7. Type **1** and press **Enter**. The final question is:

```
Do you want to:

    1) Select specific files
    2) Ignore specific files
    3) Backup up all files

Select Option: (1-3) 3
```

8. Type **3** and press **Enter**. The screen shows:

```
If you are archiving to a floppy disk drive (or other removable
media), insert a diskette.
Press the space bar to continue.
```

9. Place a formatted diskette in drive A and press **Spacebar**.

Now that the files have been archived, they can be restored if ever needed. The process is similar to archive.

10. At a workstation prompt, type **LRESTORE** and press **Enter**.

Once again you are asked a series of questions. Answer them as follows:

```
F:\INN>LRESTORE
Advanced NetWare LRESTORE V1.11 -- Archive from Local Disks
Copyright (C) 1984, 1985, 1986 Novell, Inc. All rights
Reserved.

Enter the letter of the LOCAL disk drive from which to restore
files: a

Do you wish to restore security information with the
directories? (Y/N) N

Select specific directories to be considered for
restoration? (Y/N)
(N = Consider all archived directories) N

Specify files to restore to each selected directory? (Y/N)
(N = Restore all selected directories) N

If you are restoring from a floppy disk drive (or other
    removable media), insert an archive diskette.
Press the space bar to continue.
```

11. Make sure the archive diskette is in drive A and press **Spacebar**.

Because the files on the diskette already exist in SYS:INN, you are asked to verify that you want to overwrite each one.

12. For each file, answer **Y** and press **Enter**. When finished the screen shows:

```
No more archived files on this disk.
You may do one of the following:

If you are restoring from a floppy disk drive (or other
    removable media), insert another archive diskette
    and press the space bar to continue.
Or
If you want to change drives, press the <ESC> key.
Or
If you want to end this restore session, press Ctrl/C.
```

13. Press **Ctrl-C**, then press **Enter**. The screen shows:

```
Restore session terminated.
```

14. Turn to Module 54 to continue the learning sequence.

# Module 12

## ATOTAL

### DESCRIPTION

ATOTAL is a system command valid only in NetWare versions 2.1 and above and only on networks on which the "accounting" feature has been activated (this is accomplished with SYSCON, Module 95). ATOTAL totals various network services and lists the summaries on the screen. The report includes blocks written and read, connection time by all users, disk storage (in blocks * days), and total number of service requests. You can obtain a hard copy of this report by redirecting screen output to a printer using the DOS > PRN command after ATOTAL.

### APPLICATIONS

NetWare "accounting" allows administrators to break down overall network usage among users or groups. This is useful in billing different departments for network use, as well as projecting future network needs and expansion. ATOTAL helps determine billing rates by reporting total network usage. For more information on accounting see SYSCON, Module 95.

### TYPICAL OPERATION

In this activity, you print a report of total network usage. Begin at the DOS prompt of a logged in workstation.

1. To send the report to a local printer, ensure that the local printer port is not redirected to the network—type **ENDCAP** and press **Enter**.
2. To direct the report to a network printer (in this case printer 0 on the default server), type **CAPTURE L = 0 P = 0** and press **Enter**. ENDCAP and CAPTURE are covered in Modules 34 and 17.
3. Type **ATOTAL > PRN** and press **Enter**.
4. Turn to Module 66 to continue the learning sequence.

# Module 13

## ATTACH

### DESCRIPTION

The public command ATTACH establishes a connection to a specified fileserver on multi-server networks. The fileserver's resources are made available to you (within the constraints of your user rights as established by SYSCON — see Module 95). ATTACH is similar to LOGIN (see Module 51) except that it is only used after you have logged in to a different fileserver. In other words, you must log in to a server before you can ATTACH additional servers. Also, ATTACH does not execute a login script (see Module 52) and therefore, it does not map any drives.

### APPLICATIONS

On multi-server networks you can have access to several fileservers at the same time. Use LOGIN to establish the first fileserver connection, then use ATTACH to establish additional connections.

### TYPICAL OPERATION

This activity is only valid on networks with more than one fileserver. In this activity, you LOGIN to your default server, then ATTACH a second fileserver. This activity assumes a second fileserver named ACCTG. Any other valid fileserver name can be substituted. Begin at the DOS prompt of a logged in workstation.

1. LOGIN to the default server (see Module 51).
2. Type **ATTACH ACCTG** and press **Enter**.
3. Type your username and press **Enter**.
4. If prompted, type your password and press **Enter**. (If you do not have one, you will not be prompted for one.)

You now have access to both the default and the ACCTG fileservers. Use LOGOUT (see Module 53) to detach from either or both of these fileservers.

5. Turn to Module 44 to continue the learning sequence.

# Module 14

## BINDFIX

### DESCRIPTION

The BINDFIX system command is only valid in NetWare versions 2.1 and above. Information concerning valid users, groups, fileservers, accounting, and print queues is stored in hidden files, collectively called the network *bindery*. If these files are ever corrupted, you may encounter abnormal errors. These will usually concern the inability of even supervisors to modify user or group information, or unknown fileserver errors. On the fileserver console they may specifically be referred to as bindery problems.

BINDFIX can usually repair such problems by rebuilding the bindery. BINDFIX will first make backup copies of the bindery in the SYS:SYSTEM directory. In the event of an unsuccessful attempt to BINDFIX, these backup files are used by BINDREST (see Module 15) to restore the old bindery. During the BINDFIX process certain functions will not be available to users; the administrator may want to run this process with all users logged out.

**NOTE**

> The backup bindery files are called NET$BVAL.OLD and NET$BIND.OLD. They are placed in the SYS:SYSTEM directory. After running BINDFIX, it is important not to delete these files until you are sure that the bindery has been successfully rebuilt. Without these files, BINDREST cannot restore the bindery to its previous condition. A somewhat corrupted bindery is better than a completely corrupted bindery!

In the event BINDFIX encounters user or trustee rights which should be deleted, you are prompted for permission to do so. When finished, BINDFIX reports:

```
Binder check successfully completed.
Please delete the files NET$BIND.OLD and NET$BVAL.OLD after
you have verified the reconstructed bindery.
```

You verify the new bindery by logging in and out under various usernames, printing to different print queues, and testing for appropriate trustee rights in different directories. In the event that BINDFIX is not able to reconstruct the bindery, it displays:

```
Bindery check NOT successfully completed.
```

If this occurs, or if the workstation or fileserver is interrupted during the BINDFIX process, use BINDREST (see Module 15) immediately to restore the old bindery.

## APPLICATIONS

In the event of bindery corruption, you can experience problems in executing basic NetWare operations. These problems can become steadily worse! Use BINDFIX to rebuild the bindery and restore normal network use.

## TYPICAL OPERATION

It is best *not* to run BINDFIX unless network errors indicate its necessity. If you have encountered such a need, perform the following steps. Begin at the DOS prompt of a logged in workstation.

1. Type **BINDFIX** and press **Enter**. Your display shows a list of tasks as BINDFIX performs them.
2. Turn to Module 15 to continue the learning sequence.

# Module 15

## BINDREST

### DESCRIPTION

The system command BINDREST is only valid in NetWare versions 2.1 and above. BINDREST restores the old bindery in the event that a newly constructed bindery is incomplete or otherwise unuseable. For a complete explanation of the binderies see BINDFIX, Module 14. BINDREST uses two files that BINDFIX creates prior to rebuilding the bindery. These are:

SYS:SYSTEM\NET$BIND.OLD and SYS:SYSTEM\NET$BVAL.OLD

If these files have been deleted, BINDREST will not work.

### APPLICATIONS

It is unlikely that you will need to rebuild the bindery. In the event you do, BINDFIX usually does so successfully. If, however, BINDFIX fails, it is vital that you use BINDREST to restore the old bindery. Though it may have flaws, it is better than a completely corrupted bindery!

### TYPICAL OPERATION

This activity, like the Typical Operation section of BINDFIX, should be read, but not actually performed unless you have an actual need to restore an old bindery. Begin at the DOS prompt of a logged in workstation.

1. Type **BINDREST** and press **Enter**.

Assuming that the backup files are present in the SYS:SYSTEM directory, the old bindery will be restored.

2. Turn to Module 12 to continue the learning sequence.

# Module 16
## BROADCAST

### DESCRIPTION

BROADCAST is a console command similar to SEND (see Module 84). You follow the command by a message, not enclosed in quotes, up to 60 characters in length. The message is sent to all logged in (or attached) workstations immediately. Users may block their workstations from receiving messages with the CASTOFF command (Module 18). As with the SEND command, Ctrl-Enter clears the message from your workstation.

### APPLICATIONS

Use BROADCAST to quickly send messages to all current users. This can be used by network administrators to issue global instructions such as DO NOT USE PRINTER 3 or LOGOUT ASAP.

### TYPICAL OPERATION

In this activity, you BROADCAST a message to all users currently logged in or attached to the fileserver. Begin at the : prompt of your fileserver.

1. Type **BROADCAST LOGOUT BY 5:00** and press **Enter**.
2. Turn to Module 84 to continue the learning sequence.

# Module 17

## CAPTURE

### DESCRIPTION

CAPTURE is only valid in NetWare versions 2.1 and above. Earlier versions use a very similar command called SPOOL (see Module 92). CAPTURE is a public command which redirects subsequent printer output to the specified print queue or to a specified file. During the CAPTURE process, output is temporarily stored in a *spool file*. This file is then transferred in its entirety to the queue.

Under DOS 2.x, the output is accumulated until you issue the ENDCAP command. DOS 3.x automatically sends the spooled output to the print queue when you exit the application. Either way, the spool file is automatically deleted after being sent to the queue. There are 20 flags that affect the way in which CAPTUREd output is printed. Many of them are similar to the flags used with NPRINT (see Module 63). You may use the full name or the abbreviation of each one. If you do not use flags, the defaults mentioned in the following descriptions are used.

**A** **(Autoendcap)** There are no parameters. This flag is used with DOS 2.x to force an ENDCAP (see Module 34) upon exiting an application. CAPTUREd output is then transferred to the specified queue (see Q flag) and printed. The default is Autoendcap enabled.

**B =** **(Banner = )** The parameter is text, which can be up to twelve characters and is printed on the banner page preceding the printout. The default is LST:.

**C =** **(Copies = )** The parameter is the number of copies to print. The allowed range is 0 to 255. The default is 1.

**CR =** **(Create = )** The parameter is a filename which can be preceded with a full path. When you use this flag, output is saved to the given filename as well as to the spool file. Thus, after the spool file is printed, additional printouts can be obtained by NPRINTing the CREATEd file. The default is to not create an output file.

**NOTE**

If a fileserver is specified in the path of the filename to be CREATEd, it overrides any fileserver name specified with the S flag. The CAPTUREd output is sent to the selected printer number attached to the fileserver indicated by the CREATE flag.

**F =** **(Forms = )** The parameter is a number which specifies the type of form on which the file should be printed. The allowed range is 0 to 255. Just before printing the file, the fileserver to which the target printer is attached verifies that the requested form number is the same as the last one used on that printer. If not, a message is displayed asking that the appropriate form type be loaded. Once an operator has loaded the correct form, printing is resumed by typing START PRINTER at the fileserver console and pressing Enter. The assignment of form type to form numbers is arbitrary. A list of available forms and their corresponding numbers should be established through PRINTDEF and provided to all users.

**FF** **(Form Feed)** There are no parameters. This flag restores the issuance of automatic form feeds. It counteracts the NFF flag if it was used on a previous CAPTURE command. The default is to form feed.

**J =** **(Job = )** The parameter is the name of the print job configuration you wish to use. Predefined configurations eliminate the need to specify many of the flags used with CAPTURE. For a complete explanation of print job configurations, see PRINTCON in Module 68. The default is to not use a predefined configuration.

**K** **(Keep)** There are no parameters. CAPTUREd output is held in a temporary spool file and not transferred to a print queue until the TI flag or the ENDCAP command force such a transfer. If your workstation is turned off, reset, or otherwise detached from the network before spooled output has been placed in a print queue, the output is lost. The Keep flag prevents such a loss by queueing any partial output accumulated at the time of an unexpected detachment. The default is Keep disabled.

**L =** **(Local = )** The parameter is a single-digit number indicating the local parallel printer port (LPT1: through LPT3:) which is to be redirected by the CAPTURE command. The range is 1 to 3. The default is 1.

**NA** **(NoAutoendcap)** There are no parameters. Under DOS 3.0 and above ENDCAP (see Module 34) is normally issued automatically when you exit (or enter) an application. This causes CAPTUREd output to be transferred to the specified print queue and to begin printing. The NA flag disables this action. Output remains spooled until you manually issue the ENDCAP command. The default is NoAutoendcap disabled.

**NAME =** The parameter is the username you wish to have printed on the banner page. Obviously, this flag is not valid when the NB flag is used. The default is to print your current username.

**NB** **(No Banner)** There are no parameters. Include this flag to suppress the printing of a banner page before the file is printed. The default is to print banner pages.

**NFF** **(No Form Feed)** There are no parameters. If the file being printed contains form feed commands, include this command to suppress additional automatic form feeds. The default is automatic form feeds.

**NT** **(No Tabs)** There are no parameters. This flag causes tab characters to be ignored when printing the CAPTUREd file. The default is to not ignore tabs.

**P =** **(Printer = )** The parameter indicates which printer on the indicated fileserver is the target for the files to be printed. The printer numbers are defined and can be modified with the INSTALL program (see Module 6). The range is 0 to 5, but is limited, of course, by the number of printers attached to the given fileserver. Remember, the first printer defined on a fileserver is called number zero and is the default.

**Q =** **(Queue = )** The parameter is the name of the print queue you want to receive this print job. Queues are created and modified using the console command QUEUE (see Module 74). The default is the first queue on the specified printer. If no printer, fileserver, and queue are specifed, the print job is sent to the current default server, printer 0, and queue PRINTQ_0.

**S =** **(Server = )** The parameter is a text string naming any fileserver. This server is the target for the files to be printed. If the server has more than one printer attached, you can select one with the P flag or allow the default of 0. The server chosen does not have to be one to which you are currently logged in or attached. NetWare will temporarily log in to that server, print the files, and log back out. This procedure uses the GUEST username. If a password has been assigned to GUEST, you are prompted to enter it. If the GUEST username has been deleted, you are given the opportunity to log in using any other valid username. The default is the fileserver to which you are currently logged.

**SH** **(Show)** There are no parameters. This flag causes the CAPTURE command to simply list how flag values are currently set. Use it only with no other flags.

**T =** **(Tabs = )** The parameter is the number of columns which separate the tabs in the files to be printed. The range is 0 to 18. If a file is generated by an application which does not format tabs prior to printing, this flag tells NetWare how to interpret the file. The default is 8.

**TI =** **(Timeout = )** The parameter is a number of seconds to wait after output to the spool file has ceased before issuing an automatic ENDCAP. The range is 0 to 1000. Without this flag or with a value of 0, you must exit an application everytime you want spooled output to be printed. As this can be quite an inconvenience, use this flag with a value of 10 or 15 seconds to cause timely automatic printouts. Setting the value to 0 seconds disables automatic ENDCAPs. The default is no timeouts.

## APPLICATIONS

Some software applications are designed with the ability to send output directly to network printers. When using other programs, issuing the CAPTURE command prior to entering the application can allow the easy transfer of output to any printer attached to any available fileserver.

## TYPICAL OPERATION

In this activity, you redirect printouts from LPT2: on your workstation to printer 3 on the default fileserver. Begin at the DOS prompt of a logged in workstation.

1. Type **CAPTURE L=2 P=3** and press **Enter**.

2. Now, enter any application and produce printouts as you normally would, directing them to LPT2:. They are stored in a temporary spool file. The screen should resemble the following:

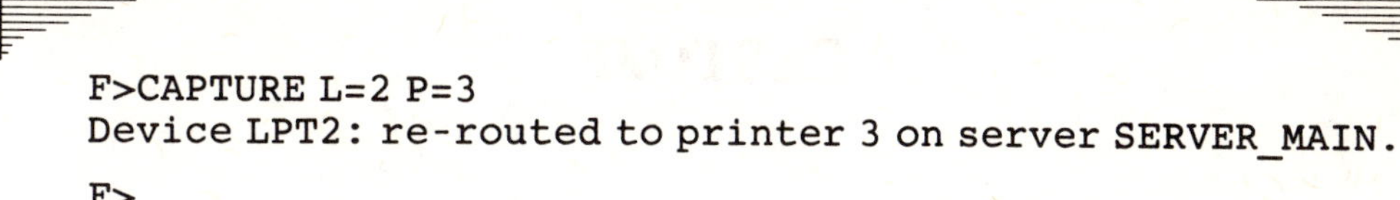

```
F>CAPTURE L=2 P=3
Device LPT2: re-routed to printer 3 on server SERVER_MAIN.

F>
```

3. Exit the application. The output from your application now begins to print on the selected network printer.
4. To display the current status of the CAPTURE flags type **CAPTURE SH** and press **Enter**.

Next use the TI flag to allow immediate printouts while in the application. Also produce two copies of the output.

5. Type **CAPTURE TI=15 C=2** and press **Enter**. Notice the display:

```
F>CAPTURE TI=15 C=2
Device LPT2: re-routed to printer 2 on server SERVER_MAIN.

F>
```

The L and P flags remain set as in step 1 until they are specifically reset in a CAPTURE command.

6. Re-enter your application and produce a printout. This time the printing begins 15 seconds later.
7. Exit your application.
8. Turn to Module 34 to continue the learning sequence.

# Module 18

## CASTOFF

### DESCRIPTION

CASTOFF is a public command that disables your workstation from receiving messages. Messages are sent to you from other workstations or a fileserver (see SEND, Modules 84 and 85, MAIL, Module 54, and BROADCAST, Module 16). The following flags can be used with CASTOFF. You can use the full names or the abbreviations. If you use a flag, follow the command CASTOFF with a forward slash (/), followed by the flag.

**A** **(All)** This flag prevents all messages (from workstations or fileservers) from being received.

**ST** **(Stations)** This flag blocks messages from other workstations only. Messages sent from a fileserver console are still received.

**T** **(Timer)** This flag does not block messages but delays the receiving of them. Normally, the workstation shell intermittently checks the network for new messages. This may cause a very brief pause in your workstation. The T flag disables this automatic network polling. With this flag set, messages are not received until your next network access.

If no flags are used, the CASTOFF command has the same effect as with the ST flag.

Use the CASTON command to re-enable message receiving (see Module 19).

### APPLICATIONS

When you are involved in an application and do not wish to be disturbed, use CASTOFF to prevent messages from being received and displayed on your screen. Because messaging is one of the advantages of a local area network, some network administrators may ask users not to use this command.

## TYPICAL OPERATION

In this activity, you disable your workstation's ability to receive messages from other workstations. Next, you verify CASTOFF's effectiveness by attempting to SEND yourself a message (see Module 85). This example assumes your username to be Fred. Substitute your actual username where you see Fred. Begin at the DOS prompt of a logged in workstation.

1. Type **CASTOFF ST** and press **Enter**. Note the display:

```
F>CASTOFF ST
Broadcast messages from other stations will now be rejected.

F>
```

2. Type **SEND "HI THERE!" TO FRED** and press **Enter**. The screen resembles this:

```
F>SEND "HI THERE!" TO FRED
Message NOT sent to SERVER_MAIN/FRED (station 3).

F>
```

3. Turn to Module 19 to continue the learning sequence.

# Module 19

## CASTON

### DESCRIPTION

The public command CASTON negates the effects of CASTOFF (see Module 18). It fully restores the ability for your workstation to receive messages. CASTON uses no flags.

### APPLICATIONS

Use CASTON to counteract the effects of the CASTOFF command.

### TYPICAL OPERATION

This activity assumes you have just completed the CASTOFF operation in Module 18. You issue the CASTON command, then SEND yourself a message (see Module 85) to verify that CASTOFF has been negated. Substitute your username where you see Fred. Begin at the DOS prompt of a logged in workstation.

1. Type **CASTON** and press **Enter**.

```
F>CASTON
Broadcast messages from other stations or the console will now
    be accepted.
Time clock broadcast checking has been enabled.

F>
```

2. Type **SEND "HI THERE!" TO FRED** and press **Enter**.

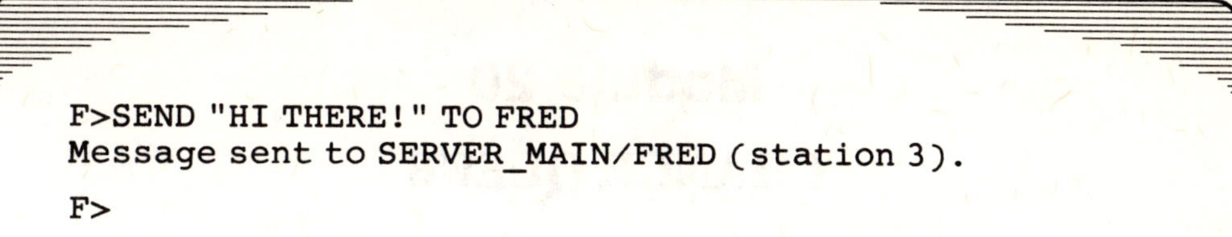

```
F>SEND "HI THERE!" TO FRED
Message sent to SERVER_MAIN/FRED (station 3).

F>
```

3. Turn to Module 96 to continue the learning sequence.

# Module 20

## CHANGE QUEUE

### DESCRIPTION

The CHANGE QUEUE console command is valid only in NetWare versions 2.0 and below. Under 2.1 and above, use the queue commands listed in Module 70. CHANGE QUEUE is used to change the order of print jobs waiting in a specified print queue. You follow the command with three numeric variables, each separated by a space. The first has a range of 0 to 4. This designates which of the fileserver's print queues is affected. The second, range 1 and above, is the number of the print job to be moved. To determine the current print job order, use the QUEUE command (see Module 73). Finally, the third variable, range 2 and above, indicates the new position for the print job in the queue. As job number 1 is the job currently being printed, job 2 is the lowest number that can be assigned.

### APPLICATIONS

Often a rush job is placed in queue behind less important jobs. Use CHANGE QUEUE to re-prioritize print jobs waiting in a print queue.

### TYPICAL OPERATION

In this activity, you change a job in print queue 0 from fifth place to second place. This example assumes that you have no jobs in the queue. Because of this assumption, your screen may vary. Begin at the : prompt of your fileserver.

1. Type **CHANGE QUEUE 0 5 2** and press **Enter**. The screen displays:

```
Priority  Job #    Directory Area     File Name
No Entries in Spool Queue 00.
Printer 00 status:  Running  On-Line  Mounted Form = 000
:
```

2. Turn to Module 94 to continue the learning sequence.

# Module 21

## CHKVOL

### DESCRIPTION

The public command CHKVOL is essentially NetWare's version of the DOS CHKDSK command but they are not interchangeable. CHKVOL reports the total amount of disk space allotted to given volumes, as well as how much space is currently available. NetWare 2.1 and above also tells you how much disk space is still available to you as a user (the network administrator can limit the amount of storage for any given user—see SYSCON, Module 95). The command can be followed by servername, volume names, and drive names, which can include the DOS wildcards, * and ?. The CHKVOL command is similar to VOLINFO (see Module 101).

### APPLICATIONS

Use CHKVOL to determine how much space is still available for use on given volumes.

### TYPICAL OPERATION

In this activity, you determine the available volume space for the current default volume. Begin at the DOS prompt of a logged in workstation.

1. Type **CHKVOL** and press **Enter**. Note the display is similar to the following:

```
F>CHKVOL
Statistics for fixed volume SERVER_MAIN/SYS:
    81547392 bytes total volume space,
    48911232 bytes in 1469 files,
    32636160 bytes available on volume,
     1233100 bytes available to user FRED.
        1263 directories available.

F>
```

2. Turn to Module 81 to continue the learning sequence.

# Module 22

## CLEAR MESSAGE

### DESCRIPTION

CLEAR MESSAGE is a console command that clears a message (as sent by SEND, Module 84) from the console screen.

### APPLICATIONS

Use CLEAR MESSAGE to eliminate messages from the console screen after reading them.

### TYPICAL OPERATION

In this activity, you clear the message "PRINTER 0 IS BROKEN!" which you sent in Module 84, SEND. Begin at the : prompt of your fileserver.

1. Type **CLEAR MESSAGE** and press **Enter**. The message at the bottom of the screen disappears.
2. Turn to Module 28 to continue the learning sequence.

# Module 23

## CLEAR STATION

### DESCRIPTION

The console command CLEAR STATION closes all files in use by the specified station. The station is essentially "knocked off" or logged out of the fileserver. You follow the command by the station number of the workstation to be cleared. The range is 1 and up. If you do not know the proper workstation, use the MONITOR command, Module 58.

### APPLICATIONS

Use CLEAR STATION to force the closure of files in use by a given workstation. This is most commonly used when the workstation cannot log out as usual.

### TYPICAL OPERATION

In this activity, you close all files and cease communication with workstation number 3. Begin at the : prompt of your fileserver.

1. Type **CLEAR STATION 3** and press **Enter**.
2. Station 3 sees the following error:

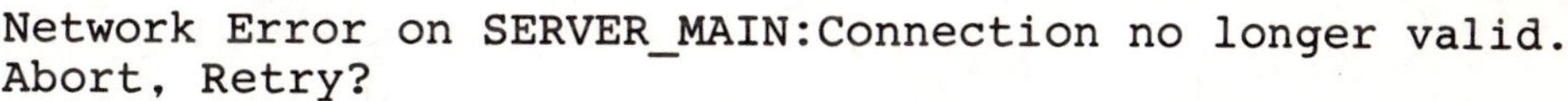

```
Network Error on SERVER_MAIN:Connection no longer valid.
Abort, Retry?
```

3. Turn to Module 32 to continue the learning sequence.

# Module 24

## CONFIG

### DESCRIPTION

CONFIG is a console command which provides information about the network interface cards that are in the fileserver. For a more complete explanation of NICs see Module 2. CONFIG lists the current node address and interrupt settings, as well as the type of NIC. Each fileserver contains between one and four NICs.

### APPLICATIONS

CONFIG is most commonly used when installing or expanding a network. As each NIC in the network must have a different node address, but should have the same interrupt setting and memory address, CONFIG can help determine how to set new NICs being added to the network. If this seems confusing, review Module 2.

### TYPICAL OPERATION

In this activity, you determine the types of NICs and their current settings, contained in the fileserver. Begin at the : prompt of your fileserver.

1. Type **CONFIG** and press **Enter**.
2. Turn to Module 58 to continue the learning sequence.

# Module 25

## CONSOLE

### DESCRIPTION

With certain versions of NetWare, fileservers can also be used as workstations. These are referred to as *nondedicated* fileservers. When a nondedicated server is booted (see Module 10), the server portion of the NetWare software is executed, then a DOS shell is loaded to allow you to run DOS applications concurrent to the server's other duties. While in this "workstation mode," console commands cannot be executed on the server. The CONSOLE command (usually located on the server's boot diskette) switches back to the "fileserver mode," allowing the use of any console command. The console command DOS (see Module 31) switches the server back to the workstation mode.

### APPLICATIONS

Use the CONSOLE command, along with the DOS command (see Module 31), to use a nondedicated server alternately as a workstation or a fileserver console. While a nondedicated server is usually left in the workstation mode, there are times when you may wish to execute console commands. This is especially true when bringing down the fileserver. As with any server, the console command DOWN (see Module 32) must be issued prior to turning off a nondedicated server.

### TYPICAL OPERATION

In this activity, you use CONSOLE to switch a nondedicated fileserver to the fileserver mode. Then you issue the console command TIME (Module 97) to display the fileserver's current date and time setting. Begin at the DOS prompt of your nondedicated fileserver.

1. Type **CONSOLE** and press **Enter**. Your screen now displays a : prompt.

Now try an example of a CONSOLE command.

2. At the : type **TIME** and press **Enter**.
3. Turn to Module 31 to continue the learning sequence.

# Module 26

## CPMOFF

### DESCRIPTION

CPMOFF is considered a system command; that is, it is located in the SYS:SYSTEM directory. CPMOFF disables a workstation's ability to open files on the network. It affects only the workstation at which it is invoked.

### APPLICATIONS

Although not a commonly used command, CPMOFF assures no further access of fileserver files until CPMON is issued or the workstation is reset. Any attempts to open NetWare files from a workstation where CPMOFF is active returns the INVALID FILE HANDLE error.

### TYPICAL OPERATION

In this operation, you disable your workstation's ability to open network files. Begin at the DOS prompt of a logged in workstation.

1. Type **CPMOFF** and press **Enter**. Note that you are returned to your DOS prompt.
2. Turn to Module 27 to continue the learning sequence.

# Module 27

## CPMON

### DESCRIPTION

This system command counteracts CPMOFF. When issued, it reinstates a workstation's ability to open NetWare files.

### APPLICATIONS

As the CPMOFF command is not often used, neither is CPMON. When a workstation is first booted, the CPMON mode is active. Like CPMOFF, CPMON affects only the workstation from which it is invoked.

### TYPICAL OPERATION

In this activity, you reinstate your workstation's ability to open network files. (This assumes you just issued the CPMOFF command in the previous module.) Begin at the DOS prompt of a logged in workstation.

1. Type **CPMON** and press **Enter**. Note that you are once again returned to your DOS prompt.
2. Turn to Module 36 to continue the learning sequence.

# Module 28

## DISABLE LOGIN

DISABLE LOGIN is a console command that locks out all workstations from logging in (see Module 51). Workstations already logged in to the fileserver are not affected by the command until they log out. This command is cancelled with ENABLE LOGIN (see Module 33).

### APPLICATIONS

Before bringing down a fileserver (see Module 32), it is important to have all workstations log out. To facilitate this process, prevent any new workstation from logging in with DISABLE LOGIN.

### TYPICAL OPERATION

In this activity, you prevent all workstations that are currently logged out from logging in to the fileserver. Begin at the : prompt of your fileserver.

1. Type **DISABLE LOGIN** and press **Enter**.

Now verify that you cannot log in to the fileserver. This example assumes your username to be FRED with the password SUNSHINE.

2. From a workstation that is not logged in, at a DOS prompt, type **LOGIN** and press **Enter**.
3. Type **FRED** and press **Enter**.
4. Type **SUNSHINE** and press **Enter** when prompted for your password. The screen displays:

```
The supervisor has disabled the login function.
F>
```

5. Turn to Module 33 to continue the learning sequence.

# Module 29

## DISK

### DESCRIPTION

The console command DISK is only valid in NetWare versions 2.1 and above. It displays various information concerning the hard disks on your network. The display is similar to the following:

```
PHYSICAL DISK STATUS AND STATISTICS
          cha    con    drv    stat   IO Err   Free   Used
00         1      0      0      OK     5        495    5
```

Following the drive number, you see the channel and controller number to which the drive is attached. Also reported is the drive's status: "OK" (no problems), "NO HOT" (Hot Fix is not running on this drive), or "OFF" (this drive is shut down). (*Hot Fix* is a feature of NetWare 2.1 and above and ELS NetWare. It detects bad disk blocks, and redirects data destined for the bad areas to a reserve of disk blocks established by NetWare for that purpose.) DISK also shows the total number of disk errors detected since installation, the number of blocks available for redirected data, and the number so far in use. The drive status will continue to be monitored until you issue the OFF command (see Module 65).

### APPLICATIONS

As a network grows, there is often a need to add new network drives. In planning such expansion, DISK provides important information about existing drives and how they are physically attached. Also DISK allows the network administrator to monitor the performance of network drives, locate defective drives, and possibly discover drives with excessive errors that are on the verge of complete failure.

## TYPICAL OPERATION

In this activity, you display the status of network drives. Begin at the : prompt of your fileserver.

1. Type **DISK** and press **Enter**. You see the "Physical Status and Statistics" display.
2. Type **OFF** and press **Enter** to clear the DISK screen.
3. Turn to Module 16 to continue the learning sequence.

# Module 30

## DISMOUNT

### DESCRIPTION

The console command DISMOUNT is used to inform NetWare that a removable volume is about to be changed. This command is only used with fileservers that use removable media as a shared device. DISMOUNT writes any cached data (that which is being held in RAM) to the removable volume and closes any open files. If the removable volume is a pack of diskettes, use the DISMOUNT PACK version of the command. With either version, follow the command with the appropriate volume number.

### APPLICATIONS

NetWare holds certain disk information in RAM memory. When changing removable media, NetWare must be informed so that appropriate data may not be written to the old disk and new information can be read from the replacement disk. Use DISMOUNT and MOUNT (see Module 59) to keep NetWare informed of such changes.

### TYPICAL OPERATION

In this activity, you prepare to remove a diskette or removable hard disk from the fileserver by telling NetWare to "shut down" the volume. If the volume being removed is a pack of diskettes, use the DISMOUNT PACK version of the command. Begin at the : prompt of your fileserver.

1. Type **DISMOUNT 1** (or **DISMOUNT PACK 1**) and press **Enter**.
2. Turn to Module 11 to continue the learning sequence.

# Module 31

## DOS

### DESCRIPTION

The console command DOS is used on nondedicated fileservers to switch from the "fileserver mode" to the "workstation mode." After you issue the DOS command (or after it is automatically issued by the boot diskette), applications can be run on the server as though it were a workstation. This only applies to versions of NetWare that allow nondedicated fileservers. For a more complete explanation of this process, see Module 25.

### APPLICATIONS

Use the DOS command, along with the CONSOLE command, to use a nondedicated fileserver alternately as a workstation or a fileserver console.

### TYPICAL OPERATION

In this activity, you return a nondedicated fileserver to the workstation mode. Begin at the : prompt of your nondedicated fileserver. (You changed to fileserver mode in Module 25.)

1. Type **DOS** and press **Enter**. Your screen now returns to a DOS prompt.
2. Turn to Module 60 to continue the learning sequence.

# Module 32
## DOWN

### DESCRIPTION

The console command DOWN prepares a fileserver to be powered off. This is the final step in "bringing down" a fileserver (see Module 10). NetWare allocates a portion of RAM memory to caching (or buffering) hard disks. This process speeds overall system performance, but it means that at any given moment crucial information may be held in RAM and not recorded to the hard disk. If the server is powered down in such a state, data can be lost or corrupted. The DOWN command tells NetWare to record all such information to disk. All workstations should be logged out of the fileserver (or at least have no active files) before you issue the DOWN command.

### APPLICATIONS

*Always* issue the DOWN command at a fileserver console before powering down the fileserver!

### TYPICAL OPERATION

In this activity, you prepare a fileserver to be powered down. Begin at the : prompt of your fileserver. Before trying this exercise, be sure that all workstations are logged out (see Module 53).

1. Type **DOWN** and press **Enter**. The screen displays:

```
:DOWN
SERVER_MAIN has been shut down. Please Re-Boot to Restart.
:
```

If there are workstations that still have active files open, the screen displays:

```
:DOWN
*** WARNING *** ACTIVE FILES OPEN. HALT NETWORK?
```

2. Type **N** to halt the DOWNing of the network. Log out the workstation(s) or use CLEAR STATION (see Module 23). Now repeat step 1.
3. Turn to Module 73 to continue the learning sequence.

# Module 33

## ENABLE LOGIN

### DESCRIPTION

ENABLE LOGIN is a console command that negates the effect of DISABLE LOGIN (see Module 28). It restores the ability for workstations to log in (see Module 51) to the fileserver.

### APPLICATIONS

After completing a task for which DISABLE LOGIN was issued, use ENABLE LOGIN to restore the server to its normal status.

### TYPICAL OPERATION

In this activity, you re-enable the ability to log in to a fileserver. You DISABLEd LOGIN in Module 28. Begin at the : prompt of your fileserver.

1. Type **ENABLE LOGIN** and press **Enter**.

Now verify that workstations can log in. This example assumes your username to be FRED and your password, SUNSHINE.

2. From a workstation that is not logged in, type **LOGIN FRED** and press **Enter**.
3. Type **SUNSHINE** and press **Enter** when prompted for a password. You are now logged in as usual.
4. Turn to Module 23 to continue the learning sequence.

# Module 34

## ENDCAP

### DESCRIPTION

ENDCAP is only valid in NetWare versions 2.1 and above. Previous versions use a very similar command called ENDSPOOL (see Module 35). ENDCAP is a public command which closes printer spool files opened with the CAPTURE command (see Module 17). These spooled files are then sent to the appropriate print queues. ENDCAP redirects subsequent printer output back to your workstation's local printer port(s).

ENDCAP need not always be issued manually. NetWare issues an automatic ENDCAP with each CAPTURE, NPRINT, LOGIN, and LOGOUT command. Under DOS 3.0 and above, ENDCAP is automatically issued each time you exit an application. This automatic feature can be disabled using the NoAutoendcap flag with the CAPTURE command. ENDCAPs are also issued automatically at specific intervals following output while you are in an application if you use the TI flag with the CAPTURE command.

There are five optional flags. You may use the full name or the abbreviation.

**ALL** This flag causes ENDCAP to release all local printer ports. This is the default.

**C** **(Cancel)** This flag causes ENDCAP to release LPT1: and delete any CAPTUREd print jobs without sending them to a print queue.

**CALL** **(Cancel ALL)** This flag has the same effect as the Cancel flag, except that it affects all local printer ports.

**CL =** **(Cancel Local = )** The parameter immediately following CL is a valid local printer port number (0-2). This flag has the same effect as the Cancel flag, except that it affects only the local printer port specified.

**L =** **(Local = )** The parameter immediately following L is a valid local printer port number (0-2). This flag cancels the CAPTURE of the specified local printer port, sending spooled output to the appropriate print queue.

## APPLICATIONS

Use ENDCAP in conjunction with CAPTURE (see Module 17) to direct printer output to network printers.

## TYPICAL OPERATION

In this activity, you close any CAPTUREd files from LPT1: and send them to the appropriate network printers. Begin at the DOS prompt of a logged in workstation.

1. Type **ENDCAP** and press **Enter**. Notice the display:

```
F>ENDCAP
Device LST: set to local mode.
F>
```

2. Turn to Module 35 to continue the learning sequence.

# Module 35

## ENDSPOOL

### DESCRIPTION

ENDSPOOL is only valid in NetWare versions 2.0 and before. Later versions use a very similar command called ENDCAP (see Module 34). ENDSPOOL is a public command which closes printer spool files opened with the SPOOL command (see Module 92). These spooled files are then sent to the appropriate printer(s). ENDSPOOL redirects subsequent printer output back to your workstation's local printer port(s).

ENDSPOOL need not always be issued manually. NetWare issues an automatic ENDSPOOL with each NPRINT, LOGIN, and LOGOUT command. Also, each time a SPOOL command is issued, NetWare first executes an ENDSPOOL command. Under DOS 3.0 and above, ENDSPOOL is automatically issued each time you exit an application. ENDSPOOLs are also issued automatically at specific intervals following output while you are in an application if you use the TI flag with the SPOOL command (see Module 92). There is one optional flag. You can use the full name or the abbreviation.

**C (Cancel)** This flag causes ENDSPOOL to cancel SPOOLed print jobs.

### APPLICATIONS

Use ENDSPOOL in conjunction with SPOOL to direct printer output to network printers.

### TYPICAL OPERATION

In this activity, you close SPOOLed files and send them to the appropriate network printers. Begin at the DOS prompt of a logged in workstation.

1. Type **ENDSPOOL** and press **Enter**. Notice the display:

```
F>ENDSPOOL
Device LST: set to local mode.
F>
```

For more complete comprehension of ENDSPOOL, repeat the Typical Operation in Module 92.

2. Turn to Module 63 to continue the learning sequence.

# Module 36

## EOJOFF

### DESCRIPTION

Each time a workstation executes a new command, an "end of job" (or EOJ) is issued. This closes any open files from the previous command. The NetWare system command EOJOFF disables this function, leaving files open until they are specifically closed by an application.

### APPLICATIONS

Certain software applications may have the need to suspend operation and issue a DOS command(s) (a process often referred to as "shelling to DOS"), then return to their previous operation. If an EOJ is issued, then needed files may be closed when the application resumes. EOJOFF prevents this automatic file closure. EOJOFF remains in effect until EOJON is issued or the workstation is reset.

### TYPICAL OPERATION

In this activity, you disable your workstation's automatic file closure. Begin at the DOS prompt of a logged in workstation.

1. Type **EOJOFF** and press **Enter**. You are returned to a DOS prompt.

**NOTE**

Remember that while in the EOJOFF mode, files must be closed by the application in use. If too many files are left open, the fileserver halts operation.

2. Turn to Module 37 to continue the learning sequence.

# Module 37

## EOJON

### DESCRIPTION

This system command counteracts EOJOFF. This means an "end of job" (EOJ) is issued with each new command executed and any open files are closed. The EOJON mode is the default.

### APPLICATIONS

When it is necessary to issue the EOJOFF command (see Module 36), it is important to disable it with EOJON as soon as possible. The EOJON mode assures automatic file closure.

### TYPICAL OPERATION

In this activity, you enable your workstation's automatic file closure (which you disabled in the previous module). Begin at the DOS prompt of logged in workstation.

1. Type **EOJON** and press **Enter**. You are once again returned to the DOS prompt.
2. Turn to Module 47 to continue the learning sequence.

# Module 38

## FCONSOLE

### DESCRIPTION

FCONSOLE is a menu-driven utility that allows you to view certain information and perform certain tasks relating to the fileserver. It is only valid in versions 2.1 and above. Some of the options are limited to users with supervisor equivalency or users that have been designated as console operators. Supervisors and console operators are created under SYSCON (Module 95). The main menu options of FCONSOLE are:

**Broadcast Console Message** This has the same effect as the console command BROADCAST (Module 16). Messages are sent to all workstations and fileservers. This selection requires supervisor privileges.

**Change Current Fileserver** This allows you to select which fileserver is your current default and log in to or log out of the fileserver. Obviously this is not used on networks with only one fileserver.

**Connection Information** This provides a list of everyone currently connected (logged in or attached) to the fileserver. If you have supervisor privileges, you can select any of these connections and view a sub-menu. Through the sub-menu you can view various information about that connection, send a message to the user at that connection, or disconnect that user from the fileserver.

**Down Fileserver** This selection has the same effect as the console command DOWN (Module 32). Through FCONSOLE, however, you can do this from any workstation. Obviously, this requires supervisor privileges.

**File/Lock Activity** This allows you to view current information about the status of files, particularly in regard to locks placed on them. This is rather technical information and is most useful to programmers. It is only available to users with supervisor privileges.

**LAN Driver Information** This displays information about the network interface card(s) installed in the fileserver. This includes NIC type, address, node, and interrupt.

**Purge All Salvageable Files** This selection has the same effect as the public command PURGE (Module 72). It ensures that any recently erased files cannot be SALVAGEd (Module 82). This requires supervisor privileges.

**Statistics** This provides a wide range of data concerning the operation of the network. Information it gives on disk usage, memory allocations, and much more can be useful to a network engineer in establishing the most efficient configuration of the network. This, too, is reserved for users with supervisor privileges.

**Status** This lists fileserver date and time, tells you if LOGIN has been disabled, and tells if Transaction Tracking System is active. (TTS is only valid in SFT NetWare.) With Supervisor status you can change any of these options.

**Version** This displays the version of NetWare currently running on the fileserver.

## APPLICATIONS

FCONSOLE combines a few features that are of use to everyone with a lot of advanced features that are of interest to supervisors, administrators, programmers, and other technically oriented individuals. The features that are useful to all users can all be duplicated with individual commands, so FCONSOLE is of greatest use to the latter group mentioned above. The technical information provided by this utility can allow a great deal of insight as to the degree of efficiency of the network. This is important both in determining the ideal configuration of newer networks, and in planning expansion of established networks.

## TYPICAL OPERATION

In this activity, you use one of the FCONSOLE selections that is available to all users to display the type of network interface card (and related information) that is in your fileserver. Begin at the DOS prompt of a logged in workstation.

1. Type **FCONSOLE** and press **Enter**. Your screen resembles this:

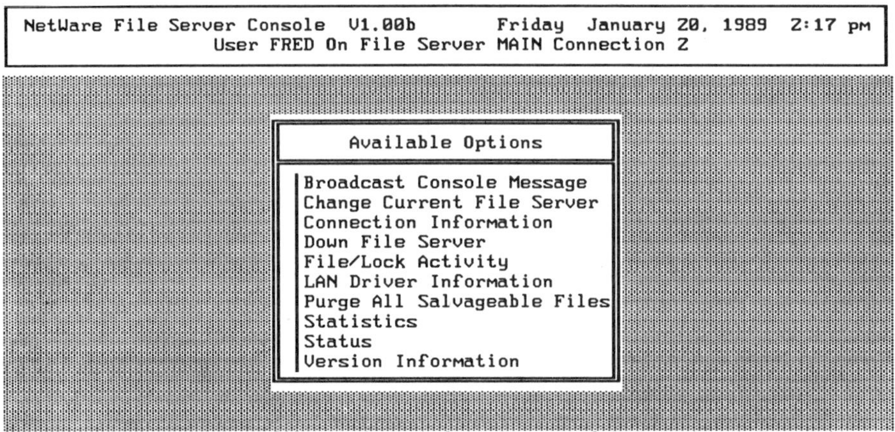


2. Press **Down Arrow** to highlight LAN Driver Information, then press **Enter**. The screen resembles the following:

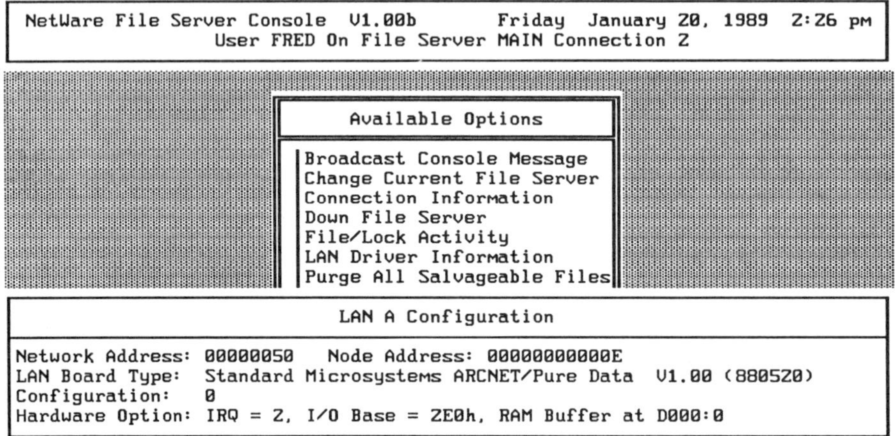


3. Exit FCONSOLE by pressing **Esc** twice, then press **Enter**.
4. Turn to Module 52 to continue the learning sequence.

# Module 39

## FILER

### DESCRIPTION

FILER is a menu-driven utility used to manage network files and directories. Most of the options available through FILER can also be accomplished with public and/or DOS commands. Because FILER is menu-driven, many users will find it to be an easier environment in which to work. While FILER is available to all users, they are restricted from file access according to established rights and trustee assignments. FILER presents the following options:

**Current Directory Information** This selection allows you to view a variety of information about the current directory. The current directory is whichever directory you were in when FILER was invoked, or the last directory selected with the Select Current Directory option below. Available information includes creation date, maximum rights mask, and a list of owners and trustees. The owner is the user who created the directory, but can be overwritten with any valid username. Trustees (users who have been assigned privileges to this directory) can be added or deleted using the Insert and Delete keys.

**File Information** This selection displays all files in the current directory. Select a given file with the arrow keys and press Enter. FILER displays information about the selected file, including attributes (e.g., READ ONLY), creation date, last accessed date, last archived date, last modified date, the owner of the file, and the size of the file in bytes. Any of this information can be changed (assuming you have the rights) except the size of file. Also, you can copy the file (as with NCOPY, Module 61) or assign it a new owner (any valid username).

Finally, you can delete any file(s) from the list. Select a file with the arrow keys, then press the Del key. You must, of course, have deletion rights to that file.

**Select Current Directory** This selection lets you select a different directory in which to work. The selection of a new current directory does not affect you when you exit FILER. In other words, the directory from which you enter FILER will always be the same as when you leave.

**Set Filer Options** This selection has eight sub-options:

**Confirm Deletions** Requires confirmation that a selected file is to be deleted. The default is to confirm.

**Confirm File Copies** This confirms each copy individually. However, FILER (as of NetWare version 2.12) doesn't support multiple file copies, so this selection has no real use.

**Confirm File Overwrites** This prevents you from accidentally copying a file to a new directory where another file with the same name already exists. In this event FILER will warn you before the copy takes place.

**Directories Exclude Pattern** This lets you specify which directories will not be included when listing directories elsewhere in FILER. On drives with a large number of directories, this can simplify your work. As you may specify multiple patterns, use the Insert and Delete keys to add or remove each pattern. Patterns may include the DOS wildcards * and ? (for example, the pattern A*.* will exclude all directories beginning with the letter A).

**Directories Include Pattern** This is exactly like the Directories Exclude Pattern option, except that specified directories will be *included* in the listings.

**File Exclude Pattern** This has the same effect on files as the Directories Exclude Pattern has on directories.

**File Include Pattern** This has the same effect on files as the Directories Include Pattern has on directories.

**File Search Attributes** This allows you to include SYSTEM and HIDDEN files in the file list. Use the Insert and Delete keys to modify.

**Subdirectory Information** This selection lists any subdirectories in the current directory. Subdirectories can be created or deleted using the Insert and Delete keys. You can display information on any subdirectory by selecting with the arrow keys and Enter. This information includes creation date, maximum rights, owner name, and current trustees. If you have the proper rights, you can change any of this information.

**Volume Information** This selection displays information about the current volume including server name, volume name, volume type, total volume size (in bytes), available bytes, total number of directory entries allowed, and number of entries still available. None of this information can be changed from within FILER.

## APPLICATIONS

FILER provides a comprehensive interface between the user and file/directory-related activities. Many users (especially novices) will find the FILER environment easy to understand and use. More experienced users may find the command equivalents of the FILER options to be quicker to envoke.

## TYPICAL OPERATION

In this activity, you use FILER to change to the directory SYS:INN, create a subdirectory named PRACTICE, and copy the file TEST.TXT into the new subdirectory. Begin at the DOS prompt of a logged in workstation.

1. Type **FILER** and press **Enter**. Your screen resembles the following:

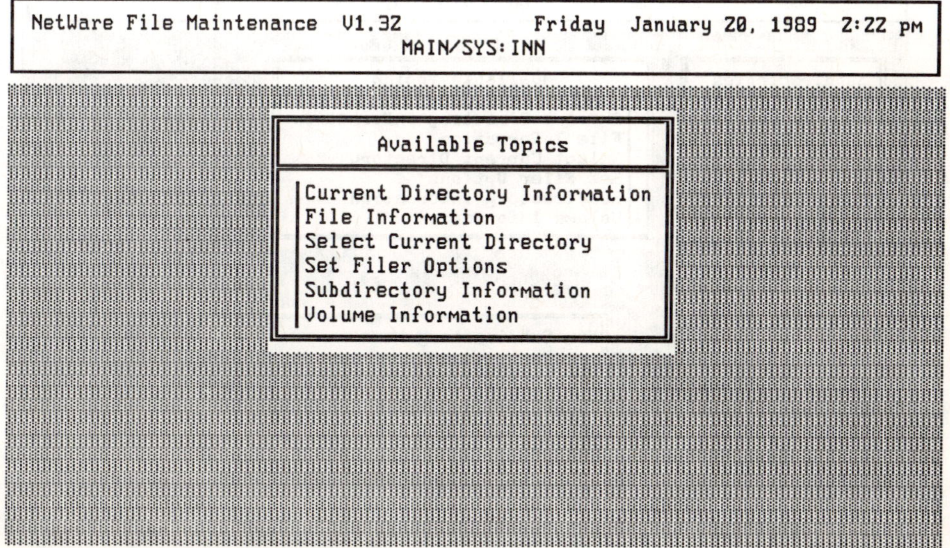

2. Press **Down Arrow** to highlight the third selection, Select Current Directory. Press **Enter**. Your screen shows:

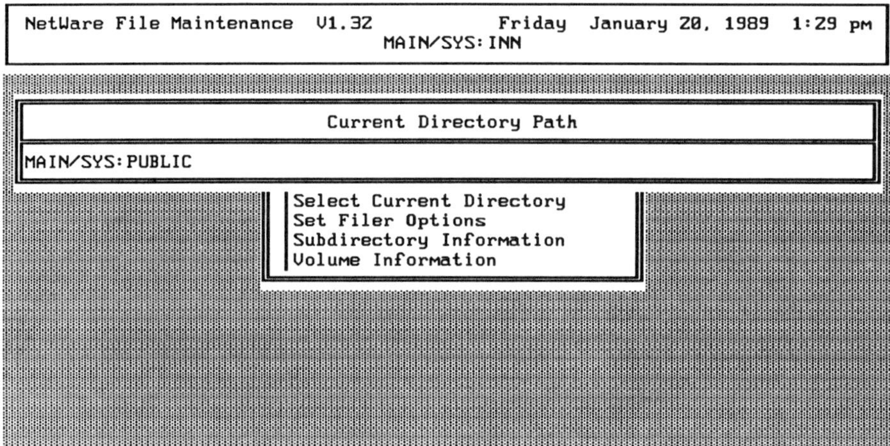


3. Press **Backspace** to delete the existing directory name, and type **SYS:INN** in its place. Press **Enter**.
4. Highlight Subdirectory Information and press **Enter**. There probably are no subdirectories, so an empty listing box is displayed.
5. Create a new subdirectory by pressing **Ins**. At this point your screen resembles the following:

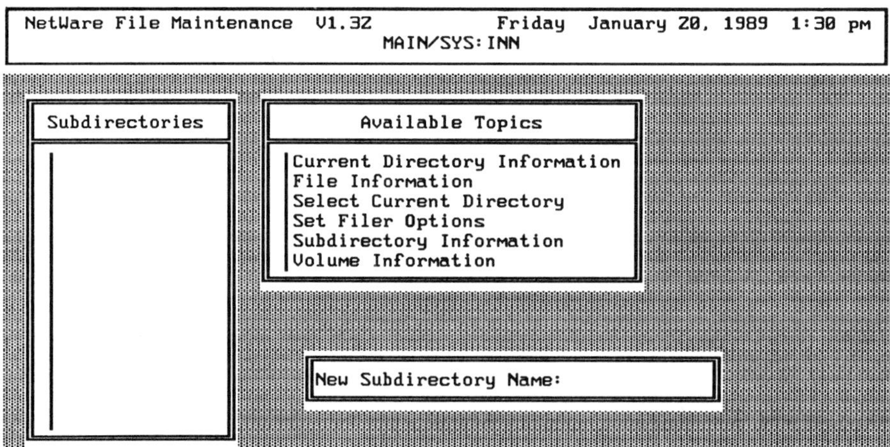

6. Type the new subdirectory name **PRACTICE** and press **Enter**. It now appears in the list.
7. Press **Esc** to return to the main FILER menu. Highlight File Information and press **Enter**. You now see a list of files in SYS:INN.
8. Highlight the file named TEST.TXT and press **Enter**. Your screen shows:

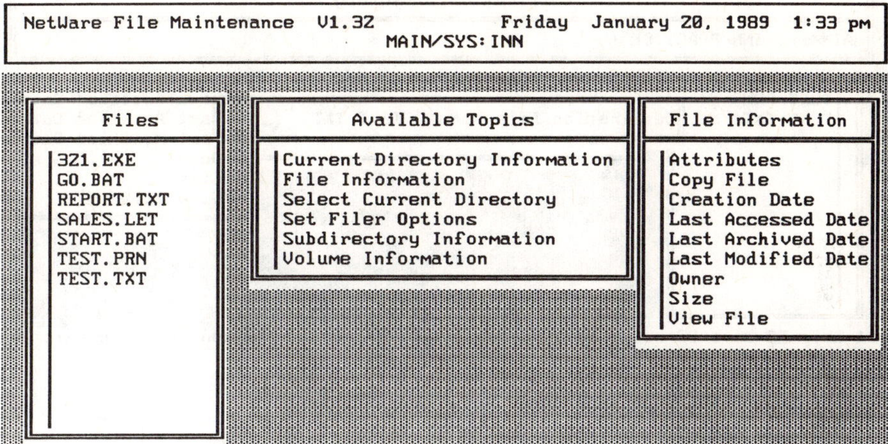


9. Highlight Copy File and press **Enter**.

You are now prompted for the name of the destination directory. Use the subdirectory you just created; you must precede it with its full path name. The name of the fileserver may be ommitted; NetWare will fill it in with the current default.

10. Type **SYS:INN\PRACTICE** and press **Enter**. At this point the screen resembles the following:

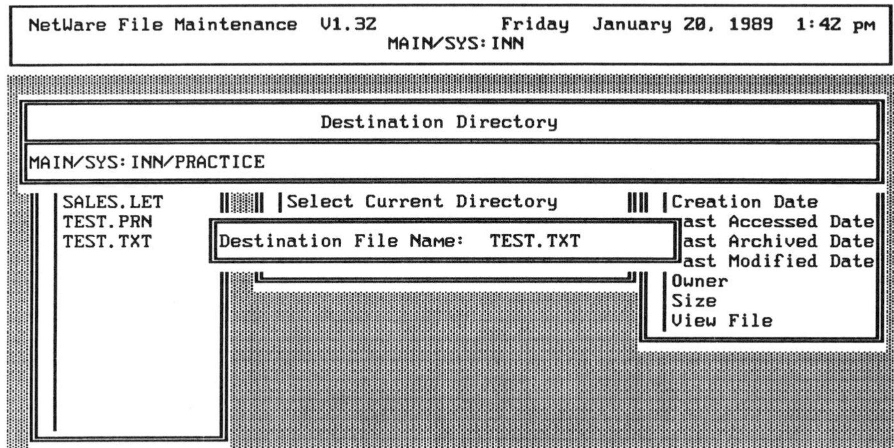


11. The name TEST.TXT is fine, so press **Enter.**
12. Press **Alt-F10** and press **Enter** to exit FILER.
13. Turn to Module 57 to continue the learning sequence.

# Module 40

## FLAG

### DESCRIPTION

FLAG is a public command used to display and/or change the attributes of specified files. The command can be followed by a complete path and filename and can include the DOS wildcards * or ?. If you do not specify a path or filename, all files in the current default directory are assumed. Unlike most NetWare commands, FLAG requires the use of at least one flag to cause a change. If you use the command alone, NetWare simply displays the current status. The following flags are used with the FLAG command. You can use the full name or the abbreviation of the flag. You must have appropriate rights to change a flag.

**N (Normal)** This flag denotes the default file attributes. These are Non-Shareable and Read/Write.

**NS (Non-Shareable)** This flag limits access to the specified file(s) to only one user at a time.

**RO (Read/Only)** This flag prevents users from modifying the specified file(s).

**RW (Read/Write)** This flag permits users to modify the specified file(s).

**S (Shareable)** This flag permits multiple users to access specified file(s) at once.

### TYPICAL OPERATION

In this activity, you display the attributes of all files in the default directory, then set them all to the Read/Write Non-Shareable status. Begin at the DOS prompt of a logged in workstation in the SYS:INN directory.

1. Type **FLAG** and press **Enter**. Your screen will resemble this:

```
F>FLAG

SERVER_MAIN/SYS:INN
   SALES.LET     Non-shareable   ReadOnly
   REPORT.TXT    Non-shareable Read/Write
   START.BAT         Shareable Read/Write

F>
```

2. Type **FLAG *.* N** and press **Enter**. Notice the display:

```
F>FLAG *.* N

SERVER_MAIN/SYS:INN
   SALES.LET     Non-shareable Read/Write
   REPORT.TXT    Non-shareable Read/Write
   START.BAT     Non-shareable Read/Write

F>
```

3. Turn to Module 62 to continue the learning sequence.

# Module 41

## FORM CHECK

### DESCRIPTION

The console command FORM CHECK is used to help align forms in a network printer. Some pre-printed forms require careful alignment so that the printout is within the spaces provided. FORM CHECK prints a row of asterisks across the page to verify form positioning. You follow the FORM CHECK command with the printer number (0 through 4) to be affected.

### APPLICATIONS

Use FORM CHECK to align such forms as continuous feed checks. Once the form is properly positioned, use FORM SET (see Module 42) to lock in the position.

### TYPICAL OPERATION

In this activity, you print an "alignment pattern" on the form loaded in printer 0 (the first printer attached to the fileserver). Begin at the : prompt of your fileserver.

1. Type **FORM CHECK 0** and press **Enter**.

A row of asterisks prints across the form in printer 0. Reposition the form and repeat step 1 until the paper is properly aligned.

2. Turn to Module 42 to continue the learning sequence.

# Module 42

## FORM SET

### DESCRIPTION

The console command FORM SET is used to "lock in" the alignment of a continuous form in the designated printer. This assures that subsequent forms are printed properly. Initial alignment can be facilitated with FORM CHECK (see Module 41). You follow the FORM SET command with the printer number (0 through 4) to be affected.

### APPLICATIONS

Use FORM SET to allow accurate printing of pre-printed forms. When a printer is out of alignment, take it off-line and issue the STOP PRINTER (see Module 94) command. Then align it, issue FORM SET, and resume printing with START PRINTER (see Module 93).

### TYPICAL OPERATION

In this activity, you "lock in" the current positioning of the form in printer 0. Begin at the : prompt of your fileserver.

1. Type **FORM SET 0** and press **Enter**.
2. Turn to Module 59 to continue the learning sequence.

# Module 43

## GRANT

### DESCRIPTION

The public command GRANT is only valid in NetWare versions 2.1 and above. GRANT is used to assign and delete rights for a given directory. You must specify a single user or group, as well as the rights you wish to grant (or deny). You also need to specify the directory if it is not the current default. This can be accomplished in a menu-driven environment using SYSCON (see Module 95). Once you have GRANTed rights to a user for a directory, that user is considered a trustee of that directory. You can only GRANT rights to directories in which you have parental rights. There are eight basic rights available:

| | |
|---|---|
| READ | DELETE |
| WRITE | PARENTAL |
| OPEN | SEARCH |
| CLOSE | MODIFY |

You can display your rights to a directory using the RIGHTS command (see Module 81). A trustee of a directory can be removed using REMOVE (see Module 76).

Follow the GRANT command by the first letter of each right which is to be changed, the directory, and the username in the following manner:

GRANT *XXX* FOR *directory name* TO *username*

Precede the initials of listed rights by "only" to clear any preexisting rights. You can also use "all but" to GRANT all rights other than those specified.

### APPLICATIONS

Use GRANT to quickly and easily allow a user or group to access a given directory. A network administrator can do this to provide access to newly created directories whose contents are of interest to the specified user or group. Users may want to share with others the contents of a directory to which the administrator has given them parental rights. While this can be done with the SYSCON menu utility, experienced users will find GRANT faster.

## TYPICAL OPERATION

In this activity, you will GRANT the user "GUEST" Read and Open rights to the SYS:INN directory (as created in Module 10). GUEST is a username which NetWare automatically creates during installation. After each of these exercises, you can verify that the command has had the desired effect by logging in as GUEST and using the RIGHTS command (see Module 81). Begin at the DOS prompt of a logged in workstation.

1. Type **GRANT R O FOR SYS:INN TO GUEST** and press **Enter.**

Now, remove these rights and GRANT only the right to Search this directory.

2. Type **GRANT ONLY S FOR SYS:INN TO GUEST** and press **ENTER.**

Finally, GRANT all rights for this directory except Delete.

3. Type **GRANT ALL BUT D FOR SYS:INN TO GUEST** and press **Enter.**
4. Turn to Module 98 to continue the learning sequence.

# Module 44

## HELP

### DESCRIPTION

HELP is a public command which provides information about the use of other NetWare commands and utilities. The HELP environment varies considerably between different versions of NetWare. It is designed to be self explanatory. You can access HELP from any directory if you are logged-in. To leave HELP press Ctrl-C.

**NOTE**

For key sequences connected by a hyphen (such as Ctrl-C), press and hold the first key while typing the second key.

### APPLICATIONS

Use HELP for quick reference to the proper use of a NetWare command.

### TYPICAL OPERATION

In this activity, use HELP to quickly review the proper use of the public command ATTACH. Begin at the DOS prompt of a logged in workstation.

1. Type **HELP** and press **Enter**. The screen looks similar to the following:

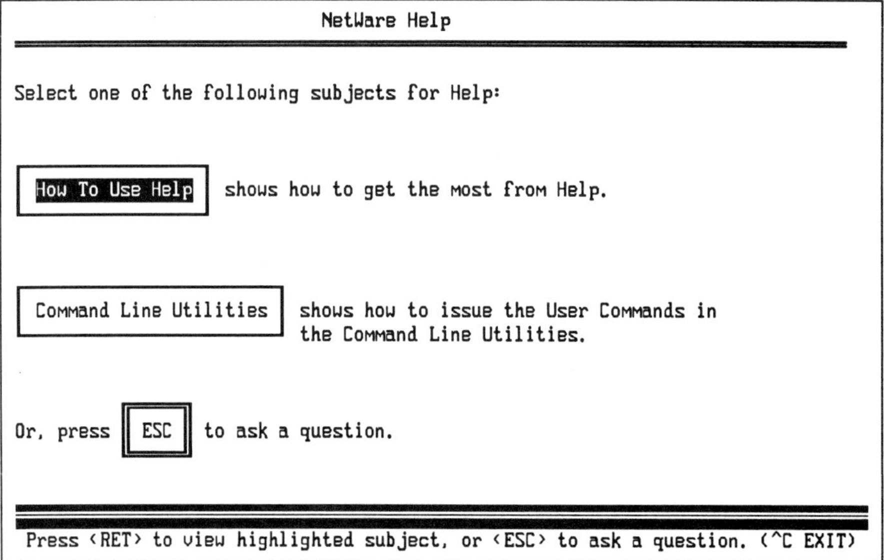


**NOTE**

This screen may vary considerably with different versions of NetWare.

2. Use the arrow keys to move the highlighted block to Command Line Utilities and press **Enter**. The screen looks similar to this:

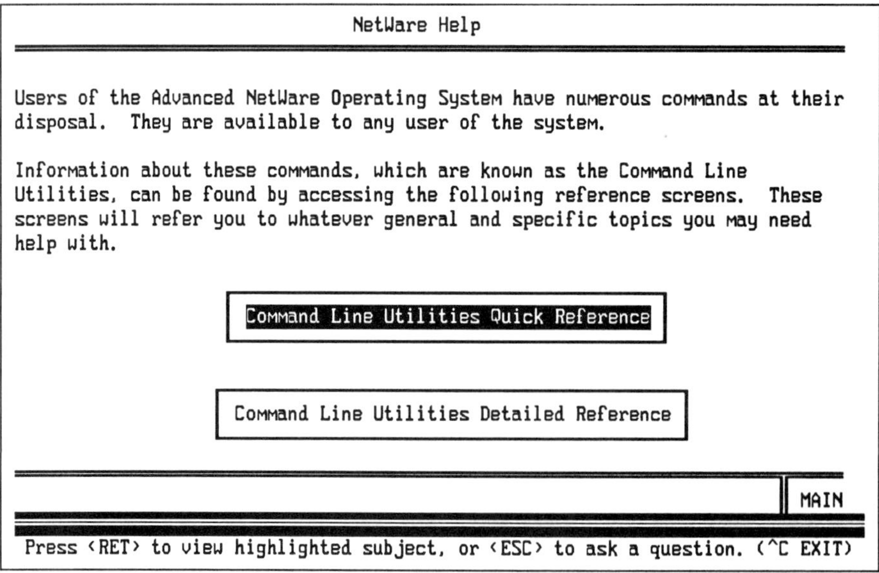

3. Highlight the "Command Line Utilities Detailed Reference" box and press **Enter**. Note the display:

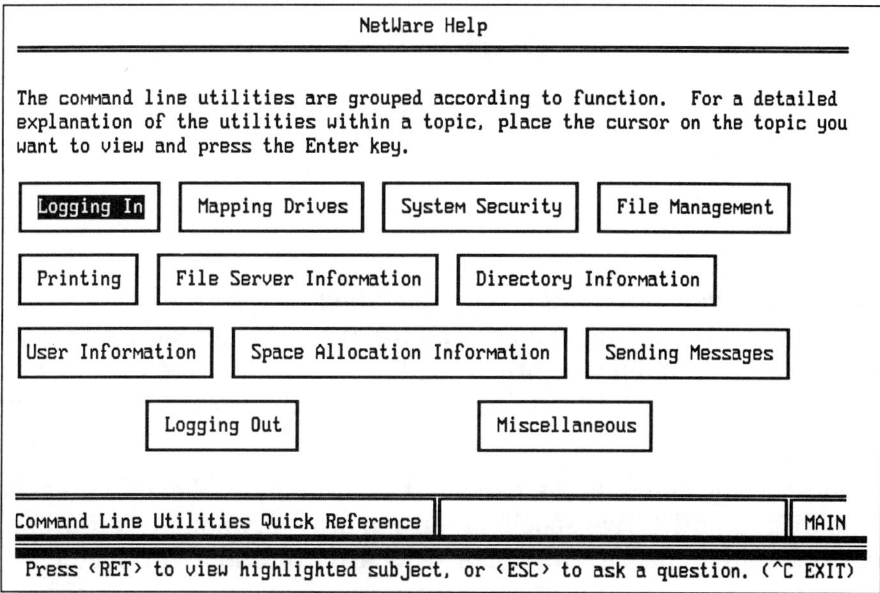


4. Press **Esc**. You now have a > prompt in the lower left corner of your screen.
5. Type **How do I send a message** and press **Enter**. The screen displays:

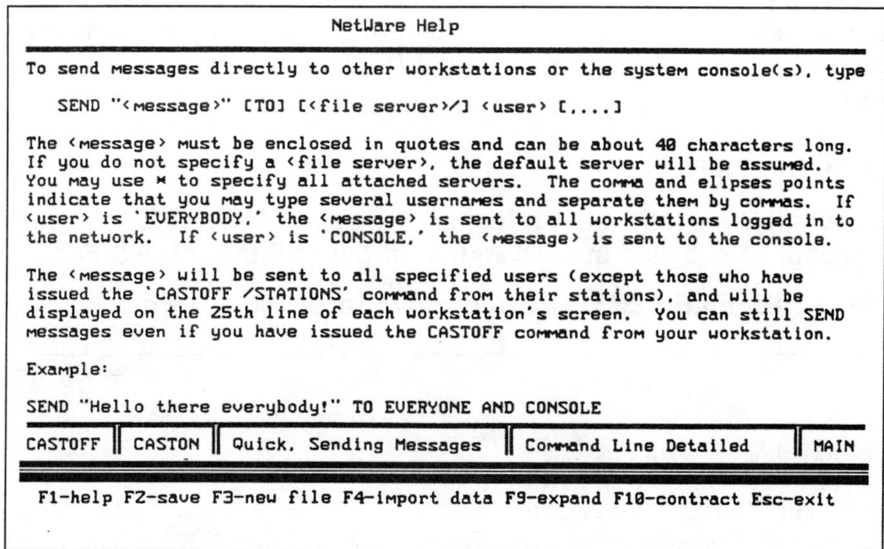


6. Press **Ctrl-C** to exit HELP.
7. Turn to Module 88 to continue the learning sequence.

# Module 45

## HIDEFILE

### DESCRIPTION

The system command HIDEFILE flags specified files so that they cannot be listed or deleted. Once hidden as such, files are no longer shown by the DOS DIR command. They cannot be erased by the DOS DELETE command, nor can they be overwritten with DOS COPY. Outside of this, however, the files are still useable.

You follow the command by the name of the file to hide. You can precede the filename with its path (drive specification and directory name) if different from the current path. You can also use wildcards (* and ?) in specifying the filename(s).

### APPLICATIONS

HIDEFILE can be used to prevent other users from knowing of a file's existence. This is a simple way of keeping certain users out of applications or data for security reasons. It is also used to protect files from being accidently erased or changed. The system command SHOWFILE restores files to their normal status (see Module 89).

### TYPICAL OPERATION

In this activity, you hide and protect a file named "TEST.TXT." Begin at the DOS prompt of a logged in workstation in the SYS:INN directory.

1. Type **HIDEFILE TEST.TXT** and press **Enter**. Note the display:

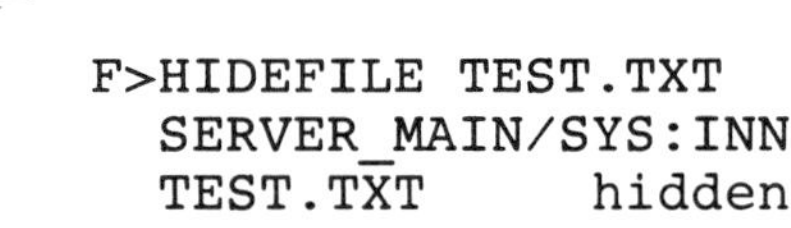

```
F>HIDEFILE TEST.TXT
  SERVER_MAIN/SYS:INN
  TEST.TXT     hidden

F>
```

2. Type **DIR TEST.TXT** and press **Enter**. Note the display:

```
F>DIR TEST.TXT

   Volume in drive F: is SYS
   Directory of F:\INN

  File not found

F>
```

3. Turn to Module 89 to continue the learning sequence.

# Module 46
## HOLDOFF

### DESCRIPTION

HOLDOFF is a system command used to release a file previously locked by HOLDON (see Module 47). It reinstates a file's ability to be accessed by several users at once. It also restores the file's ability to be printed. The syntax is HOLDOFF.

### APPLICATIONS

When you are finished using an application which was protected from other users by the HOLDON command, execute HOLDOFF.

### TYPICAL OPERATION

In this activity, you unlock a file previously locked by HOLDON (see Module 47). Begin at the DOS prompt of a logged in workstation.

1. Type **HOLDOFF** and press **Enter**. Note the display returns to your DOS prompt.
2. Turn to Module 45 to continue the learning sequence.

# Module 47

## HOLDON

### DESCRIPTION

HOLDON is a system command which locks other users out of any files that you open until you release them with HOLDOFF. Users may read these files but cannot modify them. Also, while the file is locked, it cannot be sent to the printer. The syntax is HOLDON.

### APPLICATIONS

Applications written specifically for network use allow several users simultaneous access to the same files. These programs must lock files (or records) while a given user is making changes. Otherwise the first user's changes may be overwritten by the second user. If a program is not designed to handle such data locking, and yet the program is shareable (more than one user can run the program at once), data loss or corruption can occur. By executing the HOLDON command on a program file before using it, other users cannot gain access to the file until the HOLDOFF command is issued.

Unfortunately, this also keeps you from being able to print the locked file. Therefore, you must exit the file and run HOLDOFF before printing it.

### TYPICAL OPERATION

Suppose you are on a large or spread-out network and need to use an application which is shareable, but does not provide file or record locking. To make sure that no other users access the application until you are through with it, perform the following steps. Begin at the DOS prompt of a logged in workstation.

1. Type **HOLDON** and press **Enter**. Notice the display returns to your DOS prompt.
2. Be sure to use HOLDOFF (see Module 46) to release the application to others.
3. Turn to Module 46 to continue the learning sequence.

# Module 48

## KILL PRINTER

### DESCRIPTION

The console command KILL PRINTER immediately stops output to the designated printer and deletes all jobs in its print queue. It is only valid under NetWare versions 2.0 and below. Versions 2.1 and above use the QUEUE DELETE or QUEUE DESTROY commands as described in Module 70. Additional print jobs directed to the printer accumulate in the queue and begin printing when the printer is restarted (see START PRINTER, Module 93). You follow the command with the printer number (0 through 4). If the number is omitted, printer 0 is the default and is KILLED.

### APPLICATIONS

KILL PRINTER is seldom used, as all jobs in the designated printer's queue are permanently lost. STOP PRINTER or REROUTE PRINTER (see Modules 94 and 78) are generally better commands to use. However, KILL PRINTER is effective in quickly eliminating "test" or "junk" print jobs.

### TYPICAL OPERATION

In this activity, you stop any current printouts to printer 0 and delete any jobs waiting in its print queue. Begin at the : prompt of your fileserver.

1. Type **KILL PRINTER 0** and press **Enter**.
2. Turn to Module 78 to continue the learning sequence.

# Module 49

## KILL QUEUE

### DESCRIPTION

The console command KILL QUEUE deletes a designated print job in a print queue. It is valid only under NetWare versions 2.0 and below. Under 2.1 and above, use the QUEUE DELETE command as described in Module 70. The KILL QUEUE command is followed with a printer number (0 through 4) and a print job number (1 and above). You can determine the print job number with the QUEUE command (see Modules 73 and 75).

### APPLICATIONS

Resetting the printer or even bringing down the entire network will not delete a print job which is printing or waiting in the queue. To remove an unwanted print job from the queue, use KILL QUEUE. To remove all jobs, use KILL PRINTER (see Module 48).

### TYPICAL OPERATION

In this activity, you begin sending a large print job to printer 0, then delete it. Begin at the DOS prompt of a logged in workstation.

1. Type **SPOOL TEST.TXT P=0** and press **Enter**.

Now use KILL QUEUE to delete the job as it prints.

2. At the fileserver console, type **KILL QUEUE 0 1** and press **Enter**.

The print stops immediately (or after the printer's internal buffer empties).

3. Turn to Module 48 to continue the learning sequence.

# Module 50

## LISTDIR

### DESCRIPTION

LISTDIR is a public command which lists directories which are part of the named directory. If you do not specify a directory, the current default is assumed. LISTDIR is in some ways similar to the DOS TREE command. Additional information is listed by including the following flags, separated from the command by a space and a backslash ( \ ). You can use the full names or the abbreviations.

| | |
|---|---|
| **A (All)** | This flag displays all information available with LISTDIR. This is the same as including all three of the following flags. |
| **D (Date)** | This flag displays the date and time that each listed directory was created. |
| **R (Rights)** | This flag displays your current rights or privileges in each directory (see Module 81). |
| **S (Subdirectories)** | This flag causes all directories "below" the specified directory to be included in the listing. |

### APPLICATIONS

Use LISTDIR to determine the existence and location of various directories. LISTDIR is also an easy way of determining your current rights in all directories.

### TYPICAL OPERATION

In this activity, you use LISTDIR to display all directories immediately below the current default, as well as when each directory was created. Begin at the DOS prompt of a logged in workstation.

1. Type **LISTDIR \D** and press **Enter**. The screen resembles this:

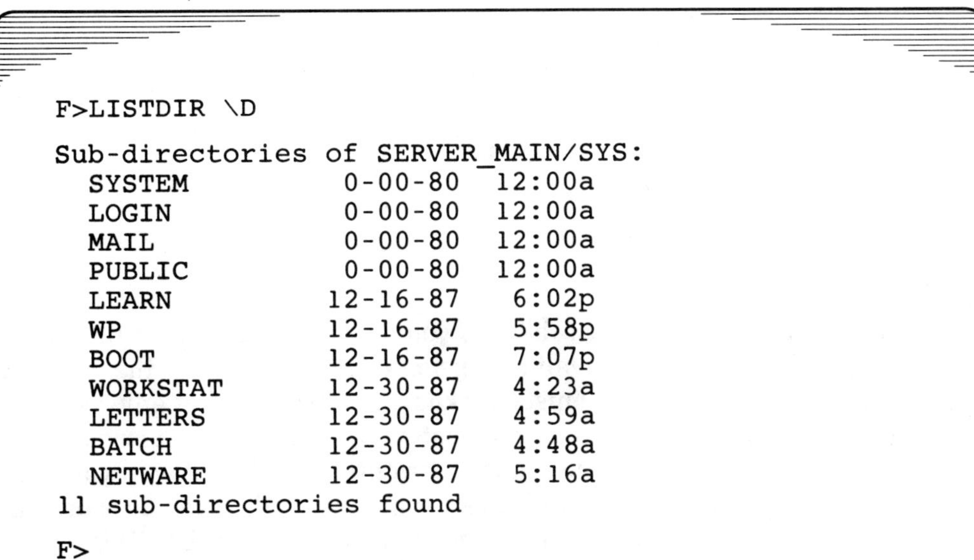

```
F>LISTDIR \D

Sub-directories of SERVER_MAIN/SYS:
  SYSTEM            0-00-80  12:00a
  LOGIN             0-00-80  12:00a
  MAIL              0-00-80  12:00a
  PUBLIC            0-00-80  12:00a
  LEARN            12-16-87   6:02p
  WP               12-16-87   5:58p
  BOOT             12-16-87   7:07p
  WORKSTAT         12-30-87   4:23a
  LETTERS          12-30-87   4:59a
  BATCH            12-30-87   4:48a
  NETWARE          12-30-87   5:16a
11 sub-directories found

F>
```

Try this command using other flags or directories as well.

2. Turn to Module 77 to continue the learning sequence.

# Module 51

## LOGIN

### DESCRIPTION

The public command LOGIN establishes you as a user on a given fileserver. You must "LOGIN" using a valid *username* as created by the network supervisor (see SYSCON). You must also know the password, if any, assigned to that username. NetWare does not distinguish between uppercase and lowercase; usernames and passwords can be entered either way. If you enter an invalid username, NetWare still asks for a password; regardless of what is entered at this point, NetWare responds with "ACCESS DENIED."

On networks with more than one fileserver, it is important to specify to which server you wish to log in. This is done by preceding the username with a valid fileserver name and a forward slash (/). To shorten this process you can enter the fileserver name (if different from the default) and the username immediately following the LOGIN command. It is possible for more than one user to have concurrent access to a fileserver using the same username. This, however, can cause confusion when listing current users and sending messages (see USERLIST and SEND).

Upon successful execution of the LOGIN command, NetWare invokes the appropriate *login script* defined by the SYSCON utility. Login scripts define search paths, and may run commands or programs in a fashion similar to the DOS *AUTOEXEC.BAT* file.

### APPLICATIONS

After booting your workstation and attaching to the network using IPX.COM and NETx.COM or ANETx.COM (see Module 10), use the LOGIN command to gain access to the files on a given fileserver. The specific files which you may access, and the ways in which you may affect them (read, write, delete, etc.) are established by the network supervisor using SYSCON. When you are finished with your work on that fileserver, use the LOGOUT command.

## TYPICAL OPERATION

In this operation, you use the LOGIN command to attach your workstation to a fileserver. This example assumes your username to be FRED, with the password SUNSHINE. Begin at the DOS prompt.

1. Boot your workstation onto the network (see Module 10).
2. Switch to the first network drive. On a typical Novell network this is drive F. Type **F:** and press **Enter**.

You are now in a directory called LOGIN which contains the file LOGIN.COM, or in versions 2.1 and above, the file is called LOGIN.EXE. Any attempt to change directories or access other files will fail until you have logged in.

3. Type **LOGIN** and press **Enter**.
4. Type **FRED** and press **Enter**.

If you have been assigned a password, you are now prompted to enter it.

5. Type **SUNSHINE** and press **Enter**. The screen resembles:

```
F>LOGIN
Enter your login name: FRED
Enter your password:

Good afternoon, FRED.

Drive A    maps to a local disk.
Drive B    maps to a local disk.
Drive C    maps to a local disk.
Drive D    maps to a local disk.
Drive E    maps to a local disk.
Drive F := MAIN/SYS:FRED
Drive U := MAIN/SYS:PUBLIC
Drive W := MAIN/SYS:WP
Drive Y := MAIN/SYS:PUBLIC
Drive Z := MAIN/SYS:PUBLIC
     -----
SEARCH1 := Z:. [MAIN/SYS:PUBLIC]

F>
```

6. Turn to Module 53 to continue the learning sequence.

# Module 52

## LOGIN SCRIPTS

### DESCRIPTION

The *login script* is a set of instructions that NetWare carries out when a user logs in. The concept is similar to that of the DOS AUTOEXEC.BAT file. You create and modify login scripts through the SYSCON menu utility (see Module 95). There is a *system login script* which is executed when any user logs in, and there are *user login scripts* which only affect the user for which they were created. The following are valid login script instructions:

**#** Place the pound sign in front of the filename for any existing command file or executable file (those with extensions of .COM or .EXE). The named file will be executed with each login. Unlike DOS AUTOEXEC.BAT files, additional files with the extension .BAT cannot be called.

**ATTACH** Use this the same way as the public command of the same name (Module 13). It allows a user to be automatically logged in to multiple fileservers.

**BREAK ON/OFF** Place this instruction at the beginning of the login script to enable (BREAK ON) or disable (BREAK OFF) the user's ability to halt the login script by using Ctrl-C or Ctrl-Break. The default is BREAK OFF.

**COMSPEC** Many applications require that DOS reload the COMMAND.COM file upon exiting them. Use the COMSPEC instruction to point to the location of this file. This prevents DOS from having to go back to the local drive from which you booted. An example of this command is:

```
COMSPEC = SYS:DOS\COMMAND.COM
```

**DISPLAY/FDISPLAY** Use this instruction to cause the contents of a specified file to be displayed at the time of login. DISPLAY is used with standard text files; FDISPLAY is used with formatted files.

**DOS BREAK ON/OFF** This is similar to the DOS command BREAK. Use DOS BREAK ON to enable the user to break out of applications by pressing Ctrl-C or Ctrl-Break. The default is DOS BREAK OFF.

**DOS SET** Use this instruction to assign values to environmental variables. It is equivalent to the DOS command SET.

**DOS VERIFY ON/OFF** Use DOS VERIFY ON to cause NetWare to verify files that are copied using NCOPY or FILER (Modules 61 and 39). Its effect is similar to that of the DOS command SET VERIFY ON used with the DOS COPY command. The default is DOS VERIFY OFF.

**DRIVE** Use this to select which will be your current drive upon logging in. An example is:

```
DRIVE G:
```

The default is the first drive on the fileserver.

**EXIT** Use this instruction to cause an immediate exit from the login script. If EXIT is followed by a filename with an extension of .EXE, .COM, or .BAT, that file will be executed.

**FIRE PHASERS** Use this strange instruction to cause a "ray gun" sound effect. The phasers can be fired up to nine times per instruction. An example is:

```
FIRE PHASERS 3 TIMES
```

**INCLUDE** Use this instruction to nest additional instructions within a login script. Put the additional instructions in a text file whose name follows INCLUDE. An example is:

```
INCLUDE SYS:INN\MORESTUFF.TXT
```

**MACHINE NAME** This assigns a machine name, as required with certain NETBIOS-compatible programs. With most applications it is not necessary.

**MAP** Use this the same way as the public command of the same name (Module 56). This instruction is usually used several times in a login script.

**PAUSE** This has the same effect as the DOS command of the same name. Operation is halted until a key is pressed.

**REMARK** This tells NetWare to ignore the balance of the instruction line. It is useful for adding comments to the login script.

**WRITE** Follow this instruction with a message, enclosed in quotes, that you want displayed at the time of login. You can also WRITE *login variable* (see the following discussion). Separate multiple messages and variables by semicolons. A semicolon at the very end of the instruction causes the WRITE to be displayed on a single line. An example is:

```
WRITE "HELLO, "; LOGIN_NAME;
```

A login script can have an "IF THEN" program control, not unlike that used in many programming languages. An example is:

```
IF LOGIN_NAME="FRED" THEN
        DISPLAY SYS:FRED\HELLO.TXT
```

LOGIN_NAME is one of 22 *login variables*. They can be used as is, or as part of a text string, if preceded with %. For example, to INCLUDE a text file called LOGIN.TXT located in a directory named after each user, you can use:

```
INCLUDE SYS:%LOGIN_NAME\LOGIN.TXT
```

The login variables are:

### User-Related Variables

**LOGIN_NAME** The username used to log in.

**FULL_NAME** The full name, if any, as assigned in SYSCON.

**NEW_MAIL** The value is *YES* or *NO* and can be checked with "IF THEN." This indicates if the user has unread mail. An example is:

```
IF NEW_MAIL="YES" THEN WRITE "YOU HAVE NEW MAIL"
```

### Workstation-Related Variables

**STATION** The workstation number.

**P_STATION** The workstation physical connection number.

**MACHINE** The type of machine for which the workstation shell was generated.

**SMACHINE** The short version of the machine name.

| | |
|---|---|
| **OS** | The operating system with which the workstation was booted. |
| **OS_VERSION** | The version of the workstation's operating system. |

**Time-Related Variables**

| | |
|---|---|
| **SECOND** | Seconds, according to the current system time. |
| **MINUTE** | Minutes, according to the current system time. |
| **HOUR** | The current hour, according to the system time. |
| **HOUR24** | The current hour in 24-hour format. (2:00 P.M. is 14:00). |
| **GREETING_TIME** | If the hour is midnight to noon, the value is *morning*; noon to 5:00 P.M. is *afternoon*, and 5:00 to midnight is *evening*. |
| **AM_PM** | The value is *AM* or *PM*. |
| **MONTH** | The current month number, 01—12. |
| **MONTH_NAME** | The name of the current month. |
| **DAY_OF_WEEK** | The day of the week, Sunday through Saturday. |
| **DAY** | The day of the month, 01—31. |
| **NDAY_OF_WEEK** | The numerical day of the week, 1 (Sun) – 7 (Sat). |
| **YEAR** | The current year in four digits. |
| **SHORT_YEAR** | The current year in two digits. |

The network administrator may not wish to let users modify their own login scripts. Novice users may have difficulty with some of the concepts used in login scripts and, therefore, may be prone to mistakes that can leave their working environment unuseable. At any rate, the system login script is only for modification by administrators and, therefore, cannot be accessed without supervisor privileges.

## APPLICATIONS

A LOGIN SCRIPT can be defined for each user according to his or her special needs. In simple networks where you use the same basic applications, USER LOGIN SCRIPTS may not be necessary. A SYSTEM LOGIN SCRIPT, giving all users the same basic working environment should suffice. However, with many networks, you may wish to map drives and search paths according to your individual needs, as well as establish login greetings according to your desires.

## TYPICAL OPERATION

LOGIN SCRIPTS are created using SYSCON and MAKEUSER (Modules 95 and 55).

Turn to Module 95 to continue the learning sequence.

# Module 53

## LOGOUT

### DESCRIPTION

The public command LOGOUT cancels your ability to access the files on a specified fileserver. This counteracts the LOGIN command and the effects of login scripts. Network access is not disabled by LOGOUT, but you are switched to the LOGIN directory on the default drive and all other drives mapped to that fileserver are no longer accessible. On single-server networks it is not necessary to specify the server name. If the server name is omitted on multi-server networks, you are logged out of all fileservers to which you had access.

### APPLICATIONS

After completing your work on a given server, use the LOGOUT command to cancel your ability to access that server's files. By logging out before leaving your workstation, you prevent others from unauthorized access of network files.

### TYPICAL OPERATION

In this activity, you release your ability to access a fileserver.

1. At the DOS prompt of a logged in workstation, type **LOGOUT** and press **Enter**. Your screen will resemble the following:

```
F>LOGOUT
FRED logged out from server SERVER_MAIN connection 1
Login  Time:  Thursday, January 12 1989   4:43 pm
Logout Time:  Thursday, January 12 1989   4:53 pm

F>
```

2. To log out of a particular fileserver, SERVER2, type **LOGOUT SERVER2** and press **Enter**.
3. Turn to Module 90 to continue the learning sequence.

# Module 54

## MAIL

### DESCRIPTION

MAIL is a utility that allows the creation, storage, sending, and receiving of memos or files. NetWare's Electronic Mail System is very advanced and yet easy to use. It has a user-friendly interface and on-line help screens. MAIL is no longer packaged with all versions of NetWare. With some of the newer versions, it must be purchased separately.

MAIL can process four types of files:

**MEMO** These are short messages to other users. Memos are created from within the MAIL utility.

**LETTER** This is used for longer messages.

**DOCUMENT** These are files created by a separate word processor.

**FILE** This can be any type of file, including executable programs and binary files.

When referring to an item of mail, always precede its name with the appropriate mail type. The mail commands are:

**CHECK** Use this command to see if any mail items have been sent to you.

**CLOSE** This puts away mail that was OPENed.

**DIRECTORY** This is used the same as the DOS command DIR. It allows you to search for files without leaving the MAIL utility.

**EDIT** This is a simple editor for creating or changing mail items.

**HELP** This provides a complete listing of MAIL commands and concepts.

**LIST** Use this command for a listing of mail items. LIST USERS or LIST GROUPS will provide a listing of available mail recipients.

| | |
|---|---|
| **OPEN** | This opens your "mailbox" and lists available items. |
| **PUT** | Use this command to copy a mail item to a file for access outside of the MAIL utility. |
| **QUIT** | This exits the MAIL utility. |
| **READ** | Use this to display the contents of a mail item. |
| **REMOVE** | This is used to delete mail items. |
| **SEND** | This command sends a mail item to the specified users. |
| **VIEW** | This allows you to read files that are not mail items without having to exit the MAIL utility. |

Once in the MAIL utility, use HELP or press F1 to review these commands and their usage.

## APPLICATIONS

The Novell Electronic Mail System is a valuable added benefit of NetWare. In fact, it is one of the main reasons some companies choose to network. Within an office, MAIL eliminates the need to pass around hand-written memos. MAIL is not only faster, but a much more organized way of processing the flow of information. The system can be used for passing quick notes, making company-wide announcements, or by the receptionist to distribute phone messages.

## TYPICAL OPERATION

In this activity, you create a memo called TEST and send it to yourself. This example uses the username FRED. Substitute your username. Begin at the DOS prompt of a logged in workstation.

1. Type **MAIL** and press **Enter**. Your screen resembles this:

```
Advanced NetWare Electronic Mail System V1.0a
Copyright (C) 1984, 1985 Novell, Inc.

No new mail.

                    Please enter a command.  Press <F1> for help.

>
```

2. Type **EDIT MEMO TEST** and press **Enter**. You now see:

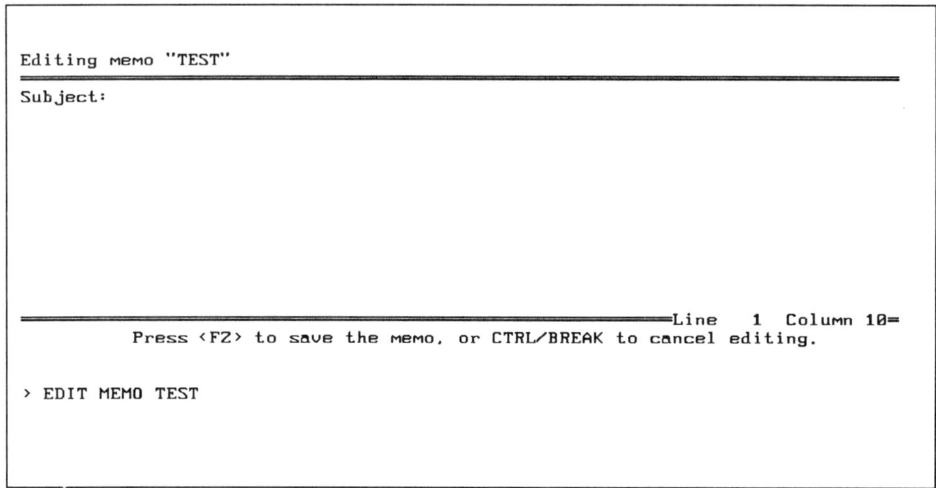


3. As the subject type **Just for practice** and press **Enter**.
4. Type **This memo is a test. I am going to send it to myself.** Press **F2** when you are finished.

5. Type **SEND MEMO TEST TO FRED** and press **Enter**. You now see:

```
Mail distribution log
════════════════════════════════════════════════════════════════════
Mail sent to user FRED









════════════════════════════════════════════════════════════════════
                           Mail distribution completed.
> EDIT MEMO TEST
> SEND MEMO TEST TO FRED
>
```

Now, check your mail and read the memo that you have received.

6. Type **CHECK MAIL** and press **Enter**. The screen looks similar to the following:

```
Newly received mail
════════════════════════════════════════════════════════════════════
  1: Memo "TEST" from FRED                     Friday, Jan 20,  3:40 pm









════════════════════════════════════════════════════════════════════
                  Please enter a command.  Press <F1> for help.
> SEND MEMO TEST TO FRED
> CHECK MAIL
>
```

7. Type **READ 1** and press **Enter**. Your memo to yourself is displayed:

```
> CHECK MAIL
>

   1: Memo "TEST" from FRED                          Friday, Feb 20,  3:40 pm
   ==========================================================================
   Subject: Just for practice

This memo is a test. I am going to send it to myself.






==========================================================================
                         Please enter a command.  Press <F1> for help.
> CHECK MAIL
> READ 1
>
```

Practice using the MAIL utility, referring to the HELP screens as needed. Finally, exit the mail system, as follows.

8. Type **QUIT** and press **Enter**. You are now returned to your workstation prompt.

Congratulations! You have completed the learning sequence.

# Module 55

## MAKEUSER

### DESCRIPTION

This utility is only valid with NetWare versions 2.1 and above and is only available to those with supervisor privileges. MAKEUSER allows you to create or delete users in batches. SYSCON (Module 95) provides an easy, menu-driven way to create users one at a time. However, if you need to create several users with similar definitions, MAKEUSER can save you a great deal of time. The MAKEUSER utility processes a text file in which a set of instructions defines the users to be created. MAKEUSER has a built-in editor for creating this file, or you can use any application that will create text files. You must give the file a .USR extension. Begin each new instruction line in the file with #. These are the valid instructions for use in a MAKEUSER file:

#### User Definition Instructions

**ACCOUNT EXPIRATION** This is used only when the SYSCON Accounting option is active. Follow the instruction by a valid date on which this user account is to expire. The default is "no expiration date."

**ACCOUNTING** This is used only when the SYSCON Accounting option is active. Follow the instruction by the opening number of accounting units available to this user, and the lowest level the account will be allowed. An example is:

```
#ACCOUNTING 5000, 0
```

**CONNECTIONS** This limits the number of workstations a user may be logged into at once. Since a fileserver has a limit of 100 concurrent connections, the values are 1-100. The default is "no limit." An example is:

```
#CONNECTIONS 2
```

**GROUPS** Follow this instruction by a list of valid GROUP names to which the user(s) will belong. An example is:

```
#GROUPS ACCTG; MNGMNT; SALES
```

**HOME DIRECTORY** This specifies a valid directory name in which to create the user(s) home directories. These directories have the same name as the username.

**LOGIN SCRIPT** This instruction tells MAKEUSER where to find a text file containing the login script to be used for the user(s) being created.

**MAX DISK SPACE** This limits the number of 4-kilobyte disk blocks that the user(s) will be allowed to use. An example is:

```
#MAX DISK SPACE 5000
```

**PASSWORD LENGTH** This instruction is only valid when preceded by the PASSWORD REQUIRED instruction. It establishes a minimum length for user passwords. The default, when a password is required, is 5.

**PASSWORD PERIOD** This, too, is only valid when preceded by the PASSWORD REQUIRED instruction. It sets the number of days between forced password changes. To force users to change their password about once a month, use:

```
#PASSWORD PERIOD 30
```

**PASSWORD REQUIRED** This instruction requires the created user(s) to use passwords.

**PURGE USER DIRECTORY** This instruction is only valid when user(s) are being deleted. It causes the subdirectories owned by the users to be deleted.

**RESTRICTED TIME** This defines times when created user(s) cannot log in to the fileserver. The term *EVERYDAY* can be used to indicate every day of the week. To keep these users out from 8:00 p.m. to midnight on Thursdays and Fridays, use:

```
#RESTRICTED TIME THURSDAY, 8:00 PM, 12:00 AM;
FRIDAY, 8:00 PM, 12:00 AM
```

**STATIONS** This limits the workstations from which users can log in to the fileserver. You must specify both network and workstation node address. These are hexadecimal numbers established at the time of network installation.

**UNIQUE PASSWORD** This is only valid when the PASSWORD REQUIRED instruction precedes it. This instruction makes created user(s) always select a password that is unique from any of the past eight passwords they have used.

**Makeuser Control Instructions**

**CLEAR** This clears all values set by the USER DEFINITION INSTRUCTIONS. Use it as follows:

```
#CLEAR
```

**CREATE** This instruction tells MAKEUSER to create a user according to any DEFINITION INSTRUCTIONS that precede. Follow CREATE by a username, full name, and passwords, separated by semicolons. To create the user FRED, with the full name of FRED FLINTSTONE and a password of DINO, you would use:

```
#CREATE FRED; FRED FLINTSTONE; DINO
```

**DELETE** This instruction tells MAKEUSER to delete a user. You can specify several users, separating their usernames with semicolons. To delete user FRED:

```
#DELETE FRED
```

## APPLICATIONS

Under NetWare 2.0 and *below*, users were created and defined one at a time. With MAKEUSER, an administrator can save a considerable amount of time by creating users with similar definitions in batches.

## TYPICAL OPERATION

This file creates users FRED SMITH and MARY SMITH with the passwords SUNSHINE and MOONLIGHT respectively. They are limited to using one workstation each at a time. They cannot use the network on Friday night. A password will always be required for these users. Begin at the DOS prompt of a logged in workstation.

1. Type **MAKEUSER** and press **Enter**. The MAKEUSER main menu appears.
2. Use the arrow keys to highlight "Create New USR File." Press **Enter**.

3. Type the following text. Press **Enter** at the end of each line.

   **#CONNECTIONS 1**
   **#RESTRICTED TIME FRIDAY, 7:00 PM, 12:00 AM**
   **#PASSWORD REQUIRED**
   **#CREATE FRED, FRED SMITH, SUNSHINE**
   **#CREATE MARY, MARY SMITH, MOONLIGHT**

   Your screen will resemble:

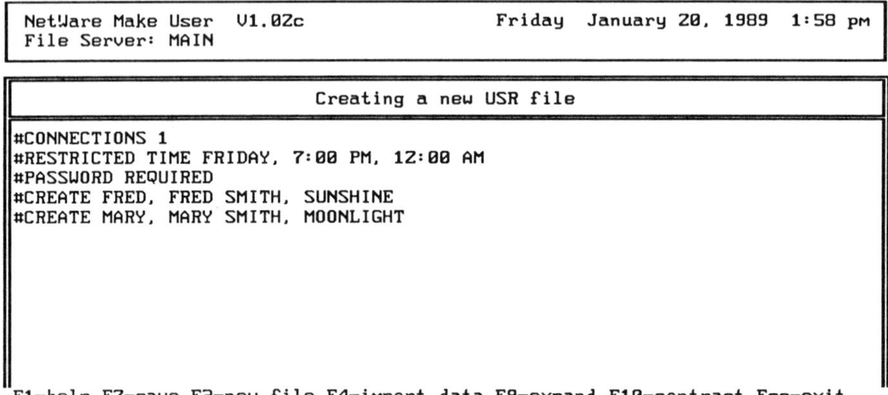


4. Press **Esc**, then type **Y** to conclude this file.

You are now prompted to enter a name for this file.

5. Type **NEWUSERS** and press **Enter**.
6. Using the arrow keys, select "Process USR File." The users are created.
7. Press **Esc**, then type **Y** to exit "Process USR File."
8. Press **Alt-F10**, then type **Y** to exit MAKEUSER.
9. Turn to Module 86 to continue the learning sequence.

# Module 56

## MAP

### DESCRIPTION

The public command MAP assigns drive names (A through Z) to NetWare directories. This command has similarities to the DOS command SUBST. A directory must have a drive name mapped to it or one of its parent directories before it can be accessed. The syntax is:

```
MAP Drive name = Vol: Directory
```

While drive names can be any letter, A-Z, you should not use letters already assigned to local drives in your workstation (such as A, for your first floppy drive). If you do, you can no longer access these local drives.

Under DOS 3.0 and above, DOS reserves drive names A-E for local use. Therefore, start with F for NetWare drive mapping. When NetWare is first installed, the default is to map the first available drive (F: under DOS 3.0 and above) to the SYS: volume's root directory. Thus, on a newly installed network with your workstation running DOS 3.0 and above, you can access the volume SYS: by typing F: and pressing Enter.

MAP can also be used to provide automatic searching through different directories for files, e.g., programs. These files must have an extension of .COM, .EXE, or .BAT. In this function, MAP is similar in effect to the DOS command PATH. When used to establish search paths, the command syntax is:

```
MAP SEARCHx: = VOL: Directory
```

SEARCH can be abbreviated with S. X is a number 1-16 that designates the order in which the directories will be searched. When you attempt to run a program, NetWare looks for it first in the current default directory, then in each SEARCH path in numerical order. If the program is not found in any of these, then the message "BAD COMMAND OR FILENAME" is displayed. Unlike the DOS PATH command, previously established search paths are not cancelled each time the command is issued.

**NOTE**

Issuing the DOS command PATH will negate any established MAP search paths and therefore should not be used. The MAP command can only designate a maximum of 26 drives. In other words, the number of drive names used plus the number of search paths established cannot exceed 26.

## APPLICATIONS

You must establish drive names before you can access NetWare directories. Even though assigning drive F: to the SYS: volume root directory will give you the ability to access its subdirectories (using the standard DOS CHDIR command), it is often more convenient to have a drive name assigned to each commonly used directory. Many users find the concept of changing drives easier to understand than that of changing directories. Map search paths allow more efficient hard disk organization. Programs can reside in one directory, yet be accessed from multiple directories. For example, a word processing program can be located in a directory called SYS:WP. Each user can have his own directory in which his documents are kept, and run the word processor from that directory.

The MAP command may be issued from a LOGIN SCRIPT (see Module 52). This will save you the trouble of typing routinely used drive mappings every time you log in. The default login script establishes search path S1 to the SYS:PUBLIC directory. This is why you can execute the public commands regardless of which directory is the current default.

## TYPICAL OPERATION

In this activity, you assign drive name P: to the directory SYS:INN. Then change the default directory to SYS:INN by changing to drive P:. Finally, verify that you are in the SYS:INN directory by running the GO.BAT program. Begin at the DOS prompt of a logged in workstation.

1. Type **MAP P:=SYS:INN** and press **Enter**. Your screen shows:

```
F>MAP P:=SYS:INN

Drive P: = MAIN/SYS:INN

F>
```

2. Type **P:** and press **Enter**.
3. Type **GO.BAT** and press **Enter**.

Now change back to drive F: and establish a search path to SYS:INN so that you can run GO.BAT without changing drives or directories. Use the search path S5, as the others already point by default to other directories.

4. Type **F:** and press **Enter**.
5. Type **MAP S5: = SYS:INN** and press **Enter**.
6. Type **GO** and press **Enter**.

This command could also be "MAP S5 = P:" since P: has been assigned to SYS:INN. NetWare will search the default directory, then any directories assigned to S1 through S4. Finally, it will find GO.BAT in the SYS:INN directory. The screen will resemble:

```
F>GO

F>DIR

 Volume in drive F is SYS
 Directory of  F:\

123           <DIR>       1-20-89   2:12p
DBASE         <DIR>       8-12-88  12:02p
WP            <DIR>       4-12-88   9:12a
FRED          <DIR>       2-12-89   2:22p
MARY          <DIR>      11-12-88   1:43p
       5 Files(s)  12199552 bytes free

F>
F>
```

Remember, these drive mappings will be lost once you log out of the network.

7. Turn to Module 91 to continue the learning sequence.

# Module 57

## MENU

### DESCRIPTION

MENU is a public command that allows you to create custom menu-driven working environments. These have the same look as SYSCON, FILER, and NetWare's other menu-driven utilities. Simply create a text file containing menu selections and the corresponding programs, and MENU will interpret it. The syntax is:

MENU *filename*

The filename normally has a .MNU extension. If a different extension is used, you must specify it when issuing the MENU command. The following is an example of the default menu provided with NetWare in the PUBLIC directory under the filename MAIN.MNU. The exact contents of the file vary between NetWare versions.

```
%Main Menu,0,0,3
1. Session Management
        Session
2. File Management
        Filer
3. Volume Information
        VolInfo
4. System Configuration
        SysCon
5. File Server Monitoring
        FConsole
6. Print Queue Management
        PConsole
7. Print Job Configurations
        PrintCon
8. Printer Definitions
        PrintDef
9. Logout
        !Logout
```

The first line is displayed at the top of the menu. It must be preceded with the %. Each menu entry is followed by the indented name of the corresponding application. This must be a filename with the extension of .EXE, .COM, or .BAT (in other words, in the above example, SYSCON refers to the program SYSCON.EXE). When invoked, this menu appears as:

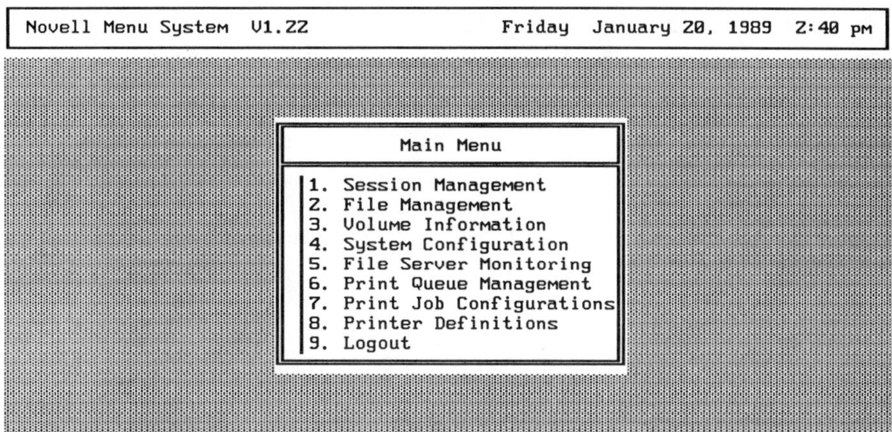


Notice that MENU puts the selections in alphabetical order.

As with all NetWare menu-driven utilities, you exit by pressing Esc until the Exit Menu box appears, then press Enter. You can also exit by pressing Alt-F10 to go directly to the Exit Menu box.

## APPLICATIONS

Many users prefer working in a menu-driven environment. This eliminates the need to memorize commands and the location of programs. Using MENU to provide a custom-built menu system, the administrator can structure the network so that users never have to issue commands from the workstation prompt.

## TYPICAL OPERATION

In this activity, you display the menu file MAIN.MNU that is located in the PUBLIC directory. This menu is not included in versions 2.0 and below. Begin at the DOS prompt of a logged in workstation.

1. Type **MENU MAIN** and press **Enter**. A menu file similar to the one at the beginning of this module appears.
2. Exit by pressing **Esc**, then press **Enter** to accept Yes to close.
3. Turn to Module 83 to continue the learning sequence.

# Module 58

## MONITOR

### DESCRIPTION

MONITOR is a console command used to monitor the activities of the fileserver and any six logged in (or attached) workstations. When you issue the command, the "monitor screen" is displayed.

Across the top, the monitor screen displays the NetWare version in use, the utilization level (a percentage of the server's processing capacity currently in use), and the disk i/o pending (or number of cache blocks waiting to be written to disk). In addition, the following information is displayed for each of the six workstations being monitored:

Station #
Current Request
The last 5 filenames accessed

The current request represents the last fileserver request made by that workstation. Common requests include:

| | |
|---|---|
| Begin transaction | Create File |
| Open File | Erase File |
| Close File | End Transaction |
| Read File | End of Job |
| Write File | |

This screen is automatically updated periodically. To force an immediate update of all activity, re-issue the MONITOR command. To exit the monitor screen, use the console command OFF (see Module 65). The MONITOR command can be followed by the number of the first station to be displayed if other than stations 1-6. The screen will display the set of six workstations which includes the specified number.

## APPLICATIONS

MONITOR provides a constant overview of network activity. The monitor screen is often left displayed while a console is not otherwise in use. Bear in mind that the constant updating of this screen takes up a small amount of fileserver processing time. MONITOR can help determine which users are accessing which files. It is useful in determining when all users have logged out in order to permit bringing down a fileserver. Also, use MONITOR to evaluate fileserver usage to determine if a given server is being too heavily accessed, thus slowing overall performance.

## TYPICAL OPERATION

In this activity, you display the monitor screen, including stations 1 through 6. Begin at the : prompt of your fileserver.

1. Type **MONITOR** and press **Enter**.

Now shift the display to include stations seven through twelve. This may be done while the existing monitor screen is still running.

2. At the : below the monitor screen, type **MONITOR 8** and press **Enter**. You see the stations 7—12 displayed.
3. Turn to Module 65 to continue the learning sequence.

# Module 59
## MOUNT

### DESCRIPTION

The console command MOUNT informs NetWare that new media has been loaded into a fileserver subsystem. This command is only used with fileservers that use removable media as a shared device. This may include certain hard disks, 8-inch floppy diskettes, and "packs" of several diskettes. In the case of disk packs, use the command MOUNT PACK. With either form of the command, follow it with the volume number.

### APPLICATIONS

NetWare holds certain disk information in RAM memory. When changing removable media, NetWare must be informed so that appropriate data can be written to the old disk and new information can be read from the replacement disk. Use DISMOUNT (see Module 30) and MOUNT to keep NetWare informed of such changes.

### TYPICAL OPERATION

In this activity, you make a newly loaded removable diskette or hard disk available to the system by informing NetWare of its presence. If the volume being loaded is a pack of diskettes, use the MOUNT PACK version of the command. Begin at the : prompt of your fileserver.

Do not perform this exercise unless you are an experienced Supervisor.

1. Type **MOUNT 1** (or **MOUNT PACK 1**) and press **Enter.**
2. Turn to Module 30 to continue the learning sequence.

# Module 60

## NAME

### DESCRIPTION

The console command NAME is used to display the name assigned to a given fileserver during the installation process (see Module 6).

### APPLICATIONS

Many NetWare commands require you to know fileserver names. On large multiserver networks, you can use the NAME command to keep track of which fileservers are which.

### TYPICAL OPERATION

In this activity, you display the name of the fileserver. Begin at the : of your fileserver.

1. Type **NAME** and press **Enter**.
2. Turn to Module 24 to continue the learning sequence.

# Module 61

## NCOPY

### DESCRIPTION

The public command NCOPY is very similar to the DOS COPY command. Because NCOPY operates on a fileserver level, without having to channel a source file through your workstation and back to the server, it is usually much faster than using DOS COPY. In naming the source and destination, you can specify the server name and directory name. If either of these is omitted, the current defaults are used. As with DOS COPY, you can use the * and ? as wildcards.

### APPLICATIONS

Use NCOPY to duplicate file(s) to a different directory, drive, or filename.

### TYPICAL OPERATION

In this activity, you make a copy of the file TEST.TXT in the SYS:INN directory. Keep the new file in the same directory, but name it NEWTEST.TXT. Begin at the DOS prompt of a logged in workstation in the SYS:INN directory.

1. Type **NCOPY SYS:INN \ TEST.TXT SYS:INN \ NEWTEST.TXT** and press **Enter**. Your screen resembles the following:

```
F>NCOPY SYS:INN\TEST.TXT SYS:INN\NEWTEST.TXT
From SERVER_MAIN/SYS:INN
To   SERVER_MAIN/SYS:INN
     TEST.TXT      to NEWTEST.TXT

     1 File copied.

F>
```

2. Turn to Module 82 to continue the learning sequence.

# Module 62

## NDIR

### DESCRIPTION

NDIR is a public command only valid in NetWare versions 2.1 and above. Under previous versions, use UDIR (see Module 99). NDIR lists files that meet given criteria. Use the command by itself to list all files in both the current directory and its subdirectories. The list includes the filename, the size (in bytes), the date and time of the last access and of the last modification to the file, the file's attributes, and the user that last modified the file. Follow the command with a partial or complete path to get a selective list of files. This path can include fileservers and volumes other than the current default, as well as the * and ? wildcard characters. The path can be followed by 25 different flags that determine which files will be listed and how they will be listed. Most of the flags have optional syntax that changes the way they are interpreted. The flags used to select files are as follows:

**ACCESS** = The parameter is a date in the form MM-DD-YY. This flag includes all files that were last accessed on the parameter date.

Options: ACCESS BEFORE, ACCESS AFTER, ACCESS NOT BEFORE, ACCESS NOT AFTER.

**CREATE** = The parameter is a date in the form MM-DD-YY. This flag includes all files that were created on the parameter date.

Options: CREATE BEFORE, CREATE AFTER, CREATE NOT BEFORE, CREATE NOT AFTER.

**DIRECTORIESONLY (Or DO)** There are no parameters. This flag includes only directories, and not files, in the list.

Options: <none>.

**FILENAME** = The parameter is a filename and can include the * and ? as wildcards.

Options: FILENAME NOT =

**FILESONLY** = There are no parameters. This flag includes files, but not directories, in the list.

Options: <none>.

**OWNER** = The parameter is a username. This flag includes all files created by this user.

Options: OWNER NOT.

**SIZE** = The parameter is a number greater than 0. This flag includes all files whose size in bytes equals this number.

Options: SIZE GREATER THAN, SIZE LESS THAN, SIZE NOT GREATER THAN, SIZE NOT LESS THAN.

**SUBDIRECTORIES (Or SUB)** There are no parameters. This flag includes all subdirectories of the current directory, but not files.

Options: <none>.

Files can also be selected based on what file attributes they have. With each of the attribute flags, you can precede the flag with the keyword "NOT." These attribute flags (and their abbreviations) include:

| | |
|---|---|
| ExecutableOnly | EO |
| Hidden | H |
| Indexed | I |
| Modified | M |
| ReadOnly | RO |
| ReadWrite | RW |
| Shareable | SHA |
| System | SY |
| Transactional | T |

Finally, there are two flags that determine how the list is displayed. The BRIEF flag lists only the filename, size, and last update for the listed files. The SORT flag sorts the list according to any of six different options. Each option can be preceded by the keyword "REVERSE" to cause the list to be sorted in reverse order. If you do not use the SORT option, files are listed in the order in which they appear in the directory. The SORT options are:

| | |
|---|---|
| **ACCESS** | Sorts on date of last access. |
| **CREATE** | Sorts on date of file creation. |
| **FILENAME** | Sorts alphabetically by filename. |
| **OWNER** | Sorts alphabetically by the username of the last user to modify the file. |
| **SIZE** | Sorts numerically by the number of bytes the file occupies on the disk. |
| **UPDATE** | Sorts on date of last file modification. |

Because this command has so many options, NetWare has provided one additional flag. This is HELP. Issue the NDIR HELP command for a review of NDIR options.

## APPLICATIONS

NDIR is an invaluable tool in setting up and organizing network directories. Because many users often use one network drive, the number of files and directories can be very large and difficult to manage with the DOS command DIR. NDIR provides a sophisticated way to list file information.

## TYPICAL OPERATION

In this activity, you use NDIR to list extensive information about the files in the directory SYS:PUBLIC. Begin at the DOS prompt of a logged in workstation.

1. Type **NDIR SYS:PUBLIC S*.*** and press **Enter**.

Now, list all the files (no subdirectories) in the SYS:PUBLIC directory that are greater than 15 kilobytes in size. Produce the list in alphabetical order according to filename.

2. Type **NDIR SYS:PUBLIC FILESONLY SIZE GREATER THAN = 15000 SORT FILENAME** and press **Enter**.
3. Turn to Module 99 to continue the learning sequence.

# Module 63

## NPRINT

### DESCRIPTION

The public command NPRINT allows you to transfer specified files directly to network printers. It is similar in concept to the DOS PRINT command. Like NCOPY, this command speeds execution by not routing the files through your workstation.

The files can reside on any available fileserver and can be sent to any network printer. You can use the * and ? wildcards in naming files to be printed. The syntax is:

```
NPRINT path\filename printer number flag
```

The following flags control the way in which the files are printed. You can use the full name, or the abbreviation of each one.

**B** = **(Banner = )** The parameter is text, which can be up to twelve characters and is printed on the banner page preceding the printout. The default is LST:.

**C** = **(Copies = )** The parameter is the number of copies to print. The allowed range is 0 to 255. The default is 1.

**D** **(Delete)** There are no parameters. If this flag is included, the specified file(s) are deleted after they are printed. The default is to not delete.

**F** = **(Forms = )** The parameter is a number which specifies the type of form on which the file should be printed. The allowed range is 0 to 255. Just before printing the file, the fileserver to which the target printer is attached verifies that the requested form number is the same as the last one used on that printer. If not, a message is displayed asking that the appropriate form type be loaded.

The assignment of form type to form numbers is arbitrary. A list of available forms and their corresponding numbers should be established and provided to all users. Under NetWare 2.1 and above, detailed information concerning form types is established using PRINTDEF.

**NB** **(No Banner)** There are no parameters. Include this flag to suppress the printing of a banner page before the file is printed. The default is to print banner pages.

**NFF** **(No Form Feed)** There are no parameters. If the file being printed contains form feed commands, include this command to suppress additional automatic form feeds. The default is automatic form feeds.

**NT** **(No Tabs)** There are no parameters. This flag causes tab characters to be ignored when printing the SPOOLed file. The default is to not ignore tabs.

**P =** **(Printer = )** The parameter indicates which printer on the indicated fileserver is the target for the files to be printed. The printer numbers are defined and can be modified with the INSTALL program (see Module 6). The range is 0 to 5, but is limited, of course, by the number of printers attached to the given fileserver. Remember, the first printer defined on a fileserver is called number 0 and is the default.

**S =** **(Server = )** The parameter is a text string naming any fileserver. This server is the target for the files to be printed. If the server has more than one printer attached, you can select one with the P flag or accept the default of 0. The server chosen does not have to be one to which you are currently logged in or attached. NetWare will temporarily log in to that server, print the files, and log back out. This procedure uses the GUEST username. If a password has been assigned to GUEST, you are prompted to enter it. If the GUEST username has been deleted, you are given the opportunity to log in using any other valid username. The default is the fileserver to which you are currently logged.

**T =** **(Tabs = )** The parameter is the number of columns which separate the tabs in the files to be printed. The range is 0 to 18. If a file is generated by an application which uses a tab character instead of the appropriate number of spaces, the flag tells NetWare how to interpret the tabs. The default is 8.

The remaining flags are only valid under NetWare 2.1 and above.

**F F** **(Form Feed)** There are no parameters. This flag will force a form feed after your document is printed. This is the default mode.

**J =** **(Job = )** The parameter is the name of the print job configuration you wish to use. Predefined configurations eliminate the need to specify many of the flags used with NPRINT. For a complete explanation of print job configurations, see PRINTCON in Module 68. The default is to not use a predefined configuration.

**NAME =** The parameter is the username you wish to have printed on the banner page. Obviously, this flag is not valid when the NB flag is used. The default is to print your current username.

**Q =** **(Queue = )** The parameter is the name of the print queue you wish to receive this print job. Queues are created and modified using the console command QUEUE (see Module 74). The default is the first queue on the specified printer. If no printer, fileserver, and queue are specifed, the print job will be sent to the current default server, printer 0, and queue PRINTQ_0.

## APPLICATIONS

Use NPRINT to quickly add files to the print queue. These files are usually generated by applications which allow you to redirect printouts to disk storage. NPRINT provides a considerable amount of control over how the files are printed.

## TYPICAL OPERATION

In this activity, you send a file named TEST.TXT located in your current directory to printer number 2 (your 3rd printer) attached to your current default fileserver. Begin at the DOS prompt of a logged in workstation in the SYS:INN directory.

1. Type **NPRINT TEST.TXT P = 2** and press **Enter.** The screen resembles this:

```
F>NPRINT TEST.TXT P=2
Queuing Data To Server SERVER_MAIN Printer 2.

SERVER_MAIN/SYS:INN
Queuing File TEST.TXT

F>
```

Next, send all files in the \INN directory with the .PRN extension to printer 0 on the current fileserver. Suppress the banner page and print two copies of each file. Printer 0 is the default, thus the P flag can be omitted.

2. Type **NPRINT \INN\ *.PRN C2 NB** and press **Enter**. The screen should resemble this:

```
F>NPRINT \INN\*.PRN C2 NB
Queuing Data To Server SERVER_MAIN Printer 0.

SERVER_MAIN/SYS:INN
      Queuing File TEST.PRN

F>
```

Finally, send a file named TEST.TXT to printer 2 on a fileserver named ACCTG. TEST.TXT is located in your current default directory. This file is to be printed on a form type number 5. Delete the file after it is printed.

3. Type **NPRINT TEST.TXT SERVER = ACCTG P = 2 F = 5 D** and press **Enter**. Note the display:

```
F>NPRINT TEST.TXT SERVER=ACCTG P=2 F=5 D
Queuing Data To Server ACCTG Printer 2.

ACCTG/SYS:
      Queuing File TEST.TXT

F>
```

4. Turn to Module 68 to continue the learning sequence.

# Module 64

## NSNIPES

### DESCRIPTION

NSNIPES is a multiuser game provided with NetWare. It is located in the PUBLIC directory. There are two versions: NSNIPES for monochrome displays, and NCSNIPES for color displays. The game allows one or more players to travel through a maze which is displayed on their monitors. Players are allowed five "lives" and score by shooting the "snipe" characters and the "factories." Movement and shooting are controlled as follows:

| | *MOVE* | *SHOOT* |
|---|---|---|
| Up | Up Arrow | W |
| Down | Down Arrow | S or X |
| Left | Left Arrow | A |
| Right | Right Arrow | D |
| Fast | Spacebar | |

Combining certain keys allows moving and shooting at 45-degree angles. To play, all players must change to the same directory and must have READ, WRITE, OPEN, and CREATE privileges in that directory.

### APPLICATIONS

Use NSNIPES to have fun!

### TYPICAL OPERATION

In this example, you play NSNIPES using the \PUBLIC directory. Each player should follow these steps, beginning at the DOS prompt of a logged in workstation.

1. Type **CD\PUBLIC** and press **Enter**.
2. If you are on a monochrome system, type **NSNIPES** and press **Enter**. On a color system, type **NCSNIPES** and press **Enter**.

The first player to complete step 2 is prompted to press Enter again to start the game. Don't start until everyone has completed step 2.

3. Press **Ctrl-Break** to quit the game. The player who started the game should be the last one to quit. Otherwise, remaining players may have to reset their workstations to quit.
4. Turn to Module 26 to continue the learning sequence.

# Module 65

## OFF

### DESCRIPTION

The console command OFF halts the MONITOR utility (see Module 58). Under NetWare versions 2.1 and above it also clears the DISK screen (see Module 29). The screen is cleared and the console display is returned to its normal state.

### APPLICATIONS

Use OFF to clear the monitor (or DISK) screen and allow the use of other console commands.

### TYPICAL OPERATION

In this activity, you clear the monitor screen which you started in the Typical Operation of Module 58. Begin at the : prompt below the monitor screen.

1. Type **OFF** and press **Enter**.

The screen clears and displays the normal console prompt (:).

2. Turn to Module 29 to continue the learning sequence.

# Module 66

## PAUDIT

### DESCRIPTION

PAUDIT is a system command and is only valid in NetWare versions 2.1 and above on which the NetWare "accounting" feature has been activated (using SYSCON, Module 95). All network activities being tracked by accounting are stored as entries in a file called SYS:SYSTEM\NET$ACCT.DAT. To conserve disk space this file is compressed, and cannot be directly read. PAUDIT reads this file and lists its information on your workstation display. If you want a hard copy of this report, use the DOS > PRN command to redirect output to the printer. After printing, you may wish to delete (perhaps after having backed up) the NET$ACCT.DAT file. If you do not, it continues to grow and can eventually waste a lot of disk space.

### APPLICATIONS

NetWare "accounting" allows administrators to breakdown overall network usage among users or groups. This is useful in billing different departments for network use, as well as projecting future network needs and expansion. This information is reported using PAUDIT.

### TYPICAL OPERATION

In this operation, you print a report of all activity on the network that accounting has been tracking. Begin at the DOS prompt of a logged in workstation.

1. To send the report to a local printer, ensure that the local printer port is not redirected to the network. Type **ENDCAP** and press **Enter.**

   To direct the report to a network printer (in this case printer 0 on the default server), type **CAPTURE L = 0 P = 0** and press **Enter**. ENDCAP and CAPTURE are covered in Modules 34 and 17.
2. Type **PAUDIT > PRN** and press **Enter** to print the report.
3. Turn to Module 97 to continue the learning sequence.

# Module 67

# PCONSOLE

## DESCRIPTION

PCONSOLE is a menu driven utility only valid in NetWare versions 2.1 and above. Previous versions use a more limited utility called QUEUE. PCONSOLE allows you to create, monitor, modify, and delete print queues. A print queue holds print jobs and sends them to the designated printer one at a time. Print jobs are sent to the print queue by NPRINT (Module 63), CAPTURE (Module 17), or by applications written specifically for network printing. PCONSOLE also allows you to add print jobs directly to a queue, delete print jobs, or rearrange the order of print jobs. The main menu of PCONSOLE offers these selections:

Change Current File Server
Print Queue Information
Print Server Information

The first selection simply allows you to choose from a list of available fileservers. The second allows you to choose from a list of existing print queues, or create and delete queues using the Insert and Delete keys. When a queue is created or selected, the following options become available:

**Current Print Job Entries** This lists print jobs waiting in this queue. Pressing Insert and Delete will add to or remove jobs from this list.

**Current Queue Status** This displays information concerning the queue, including the number of entries currently in the queue, and the number of fileservers (and print servers) attached. This also lets you enable or disable the queue's ability to accept additional print jobs, to send jobs to attached servers, and to allow additional servers to attach.

**Currently Attached Servers** This lists all fileservers currently attached to this queue. Once again, use Insert or Delete to edit the list.

**Print Queue ID** This displays the ID that is assigned to this queue.

**Queue Operators** This lists all users who have been made operators of this particular queue. Only operators and supervisors have the ability to delete and rearrange print jobs. You can Insert and Delete operators.

**Queue Servers** This lists print servers currently available to the queue. Normally, fileservers are the only print servers on the network. However, NetWare version 2.11 and above will support special dedicated print servers.

**Queue Users** This lists all users who are currently allowed to use this queue. Users or groups can be added and deleted.

The final selection is "Print Server Information." This allows you to add or delete print servers and to change their names.

## APPLICATIONS

Use PCONSOLE for comprehensive control of print queues. Any user on the network has the need to display the current contents of a queue and to delete their own print jobs (if they should decide not to print them). Users also need to view available queue names, and their corresponding printers. Only supervisors or queue operators, however, are allowed to delete anyone's jobs or make other changes to print queue information.

## TYPICAL OPERATION

In this activity, you use PCONSOLE to view the total number of print jobs currently waiting in a queue. Begin at the DOS prompt of a logged in workstation.

1. Type **PCONSOLE** and press **Enter**. Your screen shows:

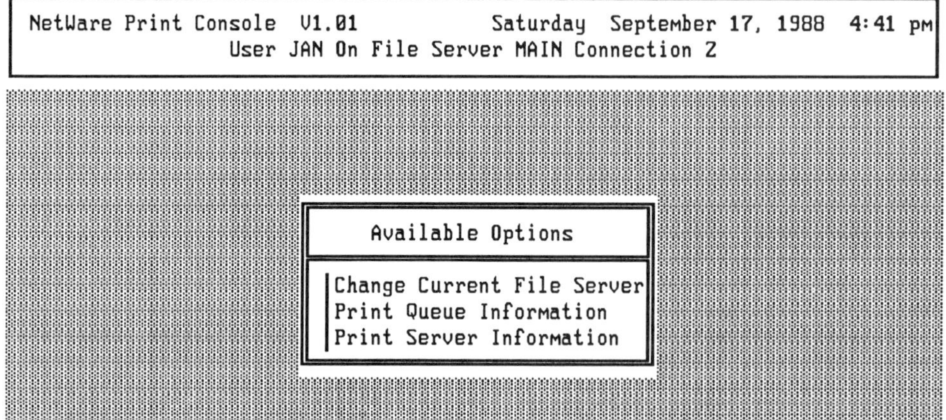

2. Press **Up Arrow** or **Down Arrow** to highlight the second selection ("Print Queue Information") and press **Enter**.
3. Highlight any print queue name and press **Enter**. The screen now shows:

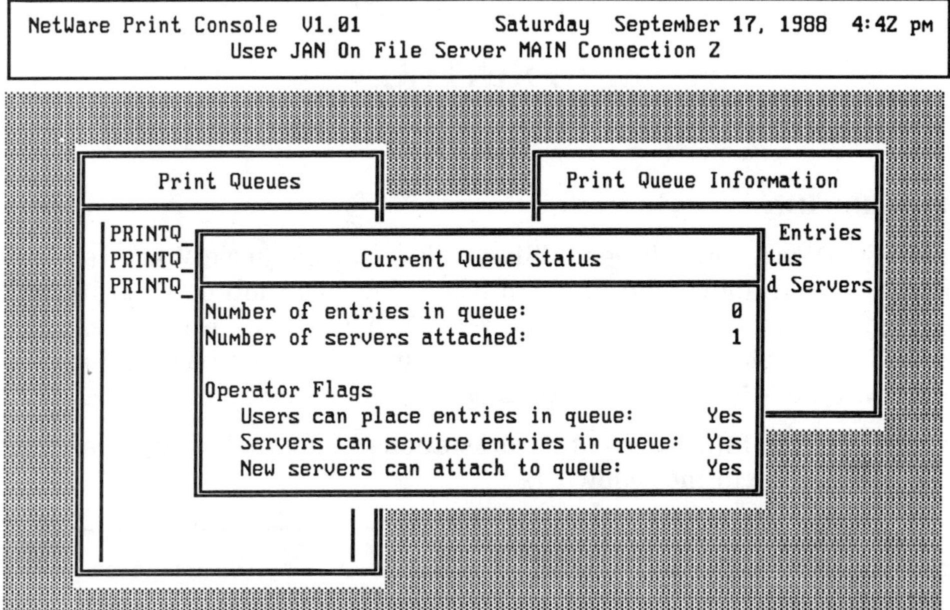


In this example, there are no print jobs waiting in this queue. Your screen may differ. Now exit PCONSOLE.

4. Press **Alt-F10**. The "Exit box" appears, then press **Enter**.
5. Turn to Module 75 to continue the learning sequence.

# Module 68

## PRINTCON

### DESCRIPTION

PRINTCON is a menu-driven utility and is only valid in NetWare versions 2.1 and above. It allows the creation of custom print job configurations. The configurations you create are only available to your username, unless a supervisor copies them to another username. They can be used for printing files with NPRINT or CAPTURE (see Modules 63 and 17).

When you type PRINTCON at a workstation prompt and press Enter, you see a menu similar to the following:

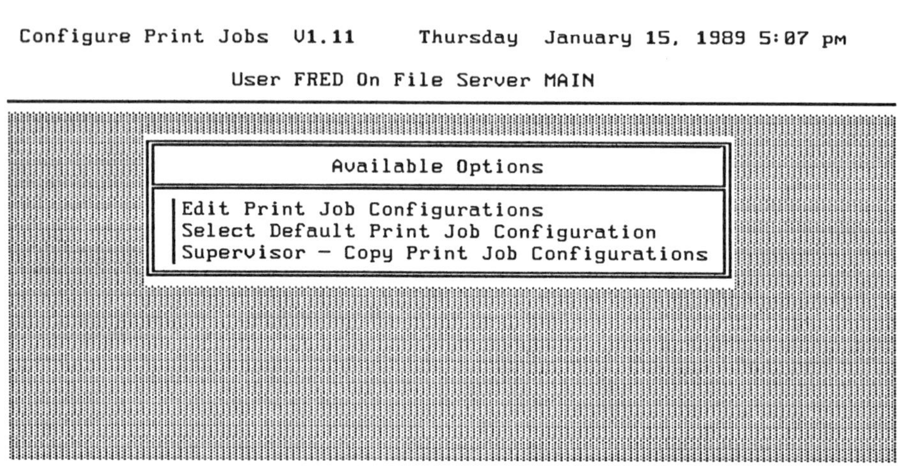


The main menu of this utility allows three options. The first, "Edit Print Job Configurations," is used to create, delete, and change print jobs. The second, "Select Default Print Job Configuration," lets you choose a print job (defined under menu option 1) to be the active one if no other job is selected when using NPRINT or CAPTURE. The last option, "Supervisor-Copy Print Job Configurations," allows a supervisor to copy one user's set of job configurations to another user. This also deletes any existing configurations for the target user. To exit PRINTCON you press Esc and type Y. You can also press Alt-F10 and type Y.

Many of the options that you can include in a job configuration are the same as the flags used with NPRINT and CAPTURE. The options and their purposes follow:

**NUMBER OF COPIES** This option determines the number of copies to print. The default is 1.

**SUPPRESS FORM FEED** This option lets you choose whether or not the printer will automatically issue form feeds. Most software will perform form feeds when necessary; therefore, setting this option to NO may cause the printer to eject extra blank pages. The default is to not suppress form feeds.

**FILE CONTENTS** This option lets you identify the type of output being printed. TEXT is considered to be an ASCII file being copied directly to the print queue (typically with NPRINT). Special format characters, such as tabs, will be interpreted. The default is TEXT.

Use BYTE STREAM when the output is coming from an application which is formatting it for the printer. In this case, NetWare assumes special characters are already interpreted.

**TAB SIZE** This option is only valid when FILE CONTENTS is set to TEXT. Use it to tell NetWare how many spaces to insert when interpreting tab characters in the output. The default is 8.

**FORM NAME** This option allows you to specify the type of form on which the file should be printed. Form names are defined in PRINTDEF (see Module 69). The default is to not use a predefined form name. Just before printing the file, the fileserver to which the target printer is attached verifies that the requested form is the same as the last one used on that printer. If not, a message is displayed asking that the appropriate form type be loaded. Once an operator has loaded the correct form, printing is resumed via the START PRINTER command at the fileserver console.

**PRINT BANNER** This option lets you choose whether or not a banner page will be printed preceding your output. The default is YES.

**BANNER NAME** This option lets you specify a username other than your own to be printed on the banner page. The default is your username.

**BANNER FILE** This option lets you specify up to twelve characters to be printed on the banner page preceding the printout. The default is the name of the file being printed.

**LOCAL PRINTER** This option, valid only with CAPTURE, is a single-digit number indicating the local parallel printer port (LPT1: through LPT3:) which is to be redirected by the CAPTURE command. The range is 1 to 3. The default is 1.

**AUTO ENDCAP** This option is only valid with CAPTURE. It forces an ENDCAP (see Module 34) upon exiting an application. CAPTUREd or SPOOLed output is then transferred to the specified queue and printed. The default is AUTO ENDCAP enabled.

**ENABLE TIMEOUT** This option causes a spooled file to automatically close and transfer to the print queue a certain number of seconds after output has ceased. If you do not ENABLE TIMEOUT, many applications will require you to exit them before printing will commence. The default is TIMEOUT *not* ENABLED.

**TIMEOUT COUNT** This option allows you to specify a number of seconds to wait after output to the spool file has ceased before issuing an automatic ENDCAP. The range is 0 to 1000. The option is meaningless unless you ENABLE TIMEOUT.

**FILE SERVER** This option lets you select a fileserver from the available list as the target for the files to be printed. The server you choose does not have to be one to which you are currently logged or attached. NetWare will temporarily log in to that server, print the files, and log back out. This procedure uses the GUEST username. If a password has been assigned to GUEST, you are prompted to enter it. If the GUEST username has been deleted, you are given the opportunity to log in using any other valid username. The default is the fileserver to which you are currently logged.

**PRINT QUEUE** This option allows the selection of the print queue you want to receive this print job. Queues are created and modified using the console command QUEUE (see Module 74). The default is the first queue on the specified printer. If no printer, fileserver, and queue are specifed, the print job will be sent to the current default server, printer 0, and queue PRINTQ_0.

**DEVICE** This option lets you select the device to which you print. The print queue selected must be assigned to this device.

**MODE** This option lets you select a print mode for your print job. Typical print modes are condensed, letter quality, elite, etc. They are defined in PRINTDEF (see Module 69).

## APPLICATIONS

PRINTCON is an important addition to NetWare 2.1. It can be a tremendous time saver and encourages the use of more print options. Any commonly used configurations should be defined and given easy-to-remember names. The administrator may want to create job configurations common to most users under a dummy username and copy the set to new users.

## TYPICAL OPERATION

In this activity, you define a print job configuration. Begin at the DOS prompt of a logged in workstation.

1. Type **PRINTCON** and press **Enter**. You see the PRINTCON menu, as illustrated in the beginning of this module.
2. Highlight the first option by pressing **Up Arrow** or **Down Arrow**, then press **Enter**. You see a list of existing configurations.

To change an existing configuration, you highlight it and press Enter. To delete one, you highlight it and press Del. When asked to confirm the deletion, you highlight "Yes" and press Enter.

3. To create a new configuration, press **Ins**. Type **TESTCON** as a name for the configuration (it could be up to 31 characters), and press **Enter.**
4. Press **Alt-F10** to exit. Highlight "Yes" and press **Enter**.
5. Turn to Module 69 to continue the learning sequence.

# Module 69

## PRINTDEF

### DESCRIPTION

PRINTDEF is available only in NetWare versions 2.1 and above. This menu-driven utility allows you to define print devices (printers and plotters) and print forms. These definitions can then be used when sending print jobs to network printers.

To define print devices, you need to provide control codes that are listed in the documentation that comes with the printer. There is a separate code for each function that the printer is capable of performing. These codes vary from printer to printer. Control codes usually start with the Esc character. Some have an obvious correlation to their purpose; the code to make an Epson FX286E printer print Emphasized is "ESC E." Many others are not so apparent; the code to make a Hewlett Packard Laserjet print in Underline is "ESC &dD."

After defining the print functions for a given print device, you can define print modes. A print mode is a combination of print functions that are called each time the mode is used. Suppose you want to define a mode to be used each time payroll checks are printed. You might include the functions "Reset" (to clear any previous functions), "LQ" (to print in letter quality), and "10CPI" (to make the printer print 10 characters per inch). The function names, such as "LQ," are arbitrary. They are any descriptive term you wish to apply when defining print device funtions.

PRINTDEF also allows you to define print forms. A print form is described, such as "3 Part NCR" or "Payroll Checks." It is then defined according to width and length. Each form definition has a unique number, within the 0-255 range.

After defining your devices and forms, you can refer to them each time you print a job. Both NPRINT and CAPTURE (Modules 63 and 17) allow you to specify the print mode and form type to be used.

The menu of PRINTDEF offers these selections:

**Print Devices**

**Edit Print Devices** This selection lists existing devices. You may use the Up Arrow and Down Arrow keys to select a device to change, or the Insert and Delete keys to create or delete devices.

PRINTDEF stores a list of functions for each device. Each function includes a descriptive name and the corresponding control codes. Edit this list as needed; use Esc to return to the main menu.

**Device Modes** This option is available once print devices have been defined. Select a print device and select, create, or delete modes using the standard menu keys (see "Edit Print Devices" above). The mode "Re-initialize" will already exist and require definition. Thereafter, create whatever other modes you need. To create a mode, assign it a descriptive name and select the appropriate functions from the provided list.

**Import Print Device** On multi-server networks, you can save time by copying print device definitions from one server to another. The first step in this process is to export the print device definition (see below). Now, ATTACH to the destination server, and re-enter PRINTDEF. Select "Import Print Device" and enter the full path name to which you exported the definition. If a definition by the same name already exists on this server, you are prompted for a new name to be assigned.

**Export Print Device** This is the first step in transferring a print device definition from one server to another. Select the device to export from the list of existing print devices. You are then prompted for a destination directory. Enter a valid complete path name. If you are exporting to a server named "ACCTG," you can enter:

```
ACCTG/SYS:PUBLIC
```

Now complete the process with Import Print Device, above.

**Forms**

You are given a list of existing forms. Select one to change, or create or delete forms using the standard menu keys. When creating a form, simply assign it a descriptive name, give it a form number (range 0 to 255), and define its length and width in lines and columns.

## APPLICATIONS

PRINTDEF allows a great range of control over network printing. Normally, the administrator defines devices and forms and informs users of their proper use. Users can use PRINTDEF for reference to view available definitions.

## TYPICAL OPERATION

In this activity, use PRINTDEF to list the print device definitions available on your current fileserver. Begin at the DOS prompt of a logged in workstation.

1. Type **PRINTDEF** and press **Enter**. The PRINTDEF main menu appears on your screen.
2. Select "Print Devices" by pressing **Up Arrow** or **Down Arrow**, then press **Enter**. Your screen shows:

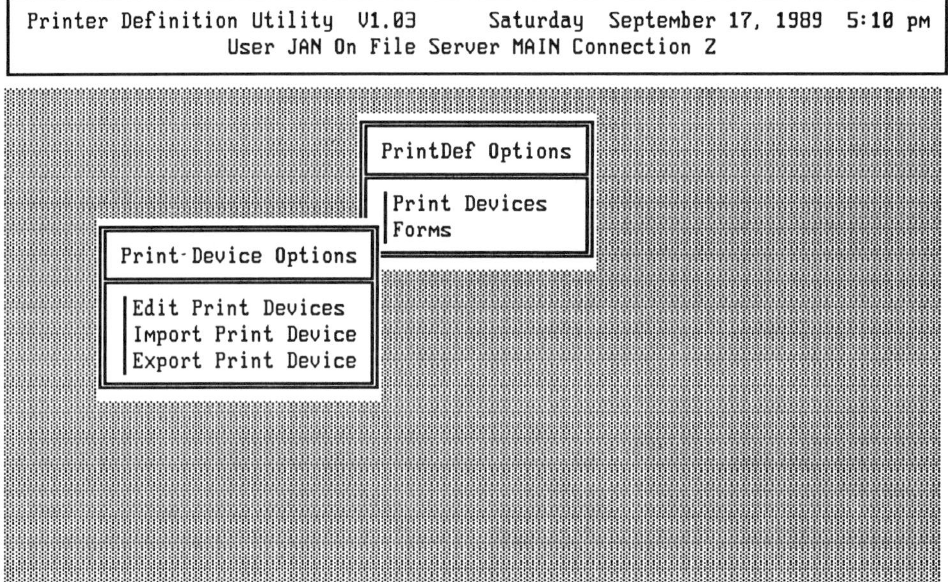


3. Select "Edit Print Devices" and press **Enter**. Your screen now lists any existing print device definitions.
4. Exit PRINTDEF by pressing **Alt-F10** and **Enter**.
5. Turn to Module 71 to continue the learning sequence.

# Module 70
## PRINTER

### DESCRIPTION

This module explains the use of 14 console commands that are related to network printing with NetWare versions 2.1 and above. Many of these commands use the keyword "PRINTER."

These commands deal with network printers that are defined with the NETGEN or ELSGEN utility (see Module 5). They also control print queues. A queue is a list of print jobs waiting to be printed. Jobs are held in the queue and sent to the appropriate printer one at a time, in the order in which they are received. Queue commands allow you to change this order, delete waiting jobs, delete entire queues, or redirect a queue to a different printer. There is always one print queue for each network printer. You can create additonal queues. Several queues may share one printer, and one queue may use several printers, passing jobs to each one as they are ready.

These are the console printer commands:

### Queue-Related Commands

**Add a Queue to a Printer** This command assigns an existing print queue to a network printer. The printer will service the queue and any others that are currently assigned according to the priority level of each queue. To add a queue called SALES to network printer 0 at the highest priority level, you use:

```
PRINTER 0 ADD QUEUE SALES AT PRIORITY 1
```

**Change a Queue's Priority** This command changes the priority of a print job within an existing print queue. If you have a rush job and there are numerous jobs waiting in the queue before you, assign your job a higher priority. To do this, you must either be a supervisor or a queue operator (see PCONSOLE, Module 67). To change a print job currently in the fifth position in a QUEUE named SALES to the first postion, use:

```
QUEUE SALES CHANGE JOB 5 TO PRIORITY 1
```

**Create a Queue** Use this command to create new queues that can then be assigned to network printers. To create a queue named SALES use:

```
QUEUE SALES CREATE
```

**Delete a Job in a Queue** This command removes a single print job from a queue. To delete job 5 from queue SALES, use:

```
QUEUE SALES DELETE JOB 5
```

**Delete All Jobs in a Queue** This command "flushes" a queue of all waiting print jobs. Use this with caution, as these jobs are completely deleted and will need to be recreated if users need them! To clear out a queue named sales, use:

```
QUEUE SALES DELETE
```

**Delete a Queue** This command doesn't delete print jobs, but simply detaches the queue from a given printer. To remove queue SALES from printer 1, use:

```
PRINTER 1 DELETE QUEUE SALES
```

**Destroy a Queue** This command deletes a queue and all jobs currently in it. Use this command with caution. To destroy queue SALES, use:

```
QUEUE SALES DESTROY
```

**List Queues on a Printer** This command lists all queues currently attached to a given printer. To view queues attached to printer 1, use:

```
PRINTER 1 QUEUES
```

**List All Queues** This command lists all queues and the printers to which they are currently attached. Simply use:

```
QUEUES
```

**List a Queue's Jobs** This command lists all print jobs currently in a given queue. To list the jobs in queue SALES, use:

```
QUEUE SALES JOBS
```

### Form-Related Commands

**Change Forms** This command tells NetWare that a new form type has been loaded into a network printer. Form types are defined with PRINTDEF (Module 69). After loading form 3 into printer 1, use:

```
PRINTER 1 FORM 3
```

**Printer Form Feed** This command simply issues a form feed to the specified printer. The paper in that printer advances one page. For printer 1, use:

```
PRINTER 1 FORM FEED
```

**Mark Top of Form** This command tells NetWare that the paper in the specified printer is now aligned at a form break. For printer 1, use:

```
PRINTER 1 MARK TOP OF FORM
```

### Other Commands

**Printers** This command displays the current status of each network printer attached to this fileserver. The printer number, queues being serviced, form currently mounted, and On-Line/Off-Line status are included in the report. Simply use:

```
PRINTERS
```

## APPLICATIONS

The PRINTER-related console commands provide the console operator a wide range of control over network printers. One of the great benefits in having a Novell network is the ability to spool printer output. With these commands the spooling procedure can be greatly enhanced. In addition to these version 2.1 commands, use STOP PRINTER, REWIND PRINTER, and START PRINTER (Modules 94, 80, and 93), to facilitate complete network printer control.

## TYPICAL OPERATION

In this activity, you create a new print queue, list all print queues, and finally, destroy the queue. Begin at the DOS prompt of a logged in workstation.

1. Type **QUEUE SALES CREATE** and press **Enter**.
2. Type **QUEUES** and press **Enter**. Note that the new queue, SALES, is listed along with any pre-existing queues.
3. Type **QUEUE SALES DESTROY** and press **Enter**.
4. To verify the deletion of this queue, you can repeat step 2.
5. Turn to Module 92 to continue the learning sequence.

# Module 71

## PSTAT

### DESCRIPTION

The public command PSTAT is only valid with NetWare versions 2.1 and above. You use PSTAT to display the status of network printers. There are two flags which can follow this command. Use the full name or the abbreviation.

**S =** **(Server = )** The parameter is any valid fileserver name on the network. PSTAT reports on the printers attached to this server. If this flag is omitted, the current default server is assumed.

**P =** **(Printer = )** The parameter is a number 0-4. It determines the printer on the specified fileserver on which PSTAT will report. If this flag is omitted, PSTAT reports on all printers attached to the fileserver.

For each printer requested, PSTAT lists the on-line or off-line status, whether the printer is active or has been stopped (using the PRINTER console command, described in Module 70), and the form type currently loaded (as defined by PRINTDEF, Module 69).

### APPLICATIONS

Use PSTAT to determine the status of network printers without having to leave your workstation. This is particularly helpful on networks with multiple shared printers. By listing the status of available printers prior to queueing print jobs (using NPRINT, CAPTURE, or SPOOL, Modules 63, 17, and 92), you can determine which printer is best suited to receive your work. If a certain printer is off-line (de-selected or turned off at the printer) or stopped at the fileserver console, you may want to use a different printer. Also if you need a particular form type, you can see if it is already loaded in a given printer.

## TYPICAL OPERATION

In this activity, you list the status of the first printer on the current default fileserver. Begin at the DOS prompt of a logged in workstation.

1. Type **PSTAT P=0** and press **Enter**. The display resembles the following:

```
F> PSTAT P=0

Server SERVER_MAIN : Network Printer Information

Printer   Ready    Status    Form: number, name
-------   -----    ------    ------------------
0         On-line  Active    1, greenbar

F>
```

Next, report on all printers attached to a fileserver named ACCT.

2. Type **PSTAT S=ACCT** and press **Enter**. The display now shows:

```
F> PSTAT S=ACCT

Server ACCT : Network Printer Information

Printer   Ready    Status    Form: number, name
-------   -----    ------    ------------------
0         On-line  Active    1, greenbar
1         On-line  Stopped   4, invoices
3         Off-line Active    5, checks1

F>
```

3. Turn to Module 67 to continue the learning sequence.

# Module 72

## PURGE

### DESCRIPTION

The public command PURGE forces the deletion of ERASEd files. The DOS ERASE (also called DEL) command appears to delete files, but actually they are only flagged for deletion. The actual deletion does not occur until any command is executed from your workstation which creates or deletes other files, or until the PURGE command is issued. The syntax is simply:

```
PURGE
```

If you issue an ERASE command which affects files that you did not mean to delete, you can un-ERASE them using the SALVAGE command (see Module 82).

### APPLICATIONS

The PURGE command is used to permanently delete files which have been ERASEd.

### TYPICAL OPERATION

In this activity, you mark a file named TEST.NEW for deletion using the DOS ERASE command. Next, you complete the deletion process using PURGE. Start by creating TEST.NEW using the DOS COPY command and the file TEST.TXT, created in Module 10. Begin at the DOS prompt of a logged in workstation.

1. Type **CD\INN** and press **Enter**.
2. Type **COPY TEST.TXT  TEST.NEW** and press **Enter**. The screen reports:

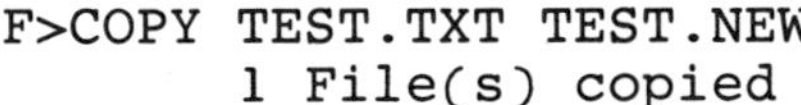

```
F>COPY TEST.TXT TEST.NEW
      1 File(s) copied

F>
```

3. Type **ERASE TEST.NEW** and press **Enter**.

At this point the file appears to be deleted. A directory listing will not include it. However, it could be restored using the SALVAGE command.

4. Type **PURGE** and press **Enter**. The file is now permanently deleted and the following prompt appears:

```
F>ERASE TEST.TXT

F>PURGE
All your recoverable erased files have been purged from the
network.
F>
```

Verify the purging of TEST.NEW using SALVAGE (Module 82).

5. Type **SALVAGE** and press **Enter**. The screen displays:

```
F>SALVAGE
Salvaging files on volume MAIN/SYS:
No files recovered.

F>
```

6. Turn to Module 17 to continue the learning sequence.

# Module 73

## QUEUE (CONSOLE 2.1)

### DESCRIPTION

There are several console commands beginning with the keyword QUEUE that are only valid under NetWare versions 2.1 and above. They allow the creation, deletion, and redirection of print queues, as well as the jobs contained in these queues. These commands are discussed in Module 70.

Turn to Module 70 to continue the learning sequence.

# Module 74

## QUEUE (CONSOLE)

### DESCRIPTION

The console command QUEUE is valid under NetWare versions 2.0 and below. Versions 2.1 and above provide the QUEUES and PRINTERS commands in Module 70 to accomplish similar results. QUEUE displays current information about a given print queue. For a more detailed explanation of print queues see QUEUE (Public), Module 75. Queue lists all print jobs waiting for the specified printer, and displays the printer's status (on- or off-line) and the form number currently loaded. Form numbers are assigned by the network administrator (using the PRINTDEF command) and selected by the public commands SPOOL, CAPTURE, and NPRINT (see Modules 92, 17, and 63). You follow the QUEUE command with the fileserver printer number (0 through 4).

### APPLICATIONS

Use QUEUE to check the condition of a printer (on-line or off-line) as well as which form type is loaded. Also use QUEUE to determine the order of print jobs and their assigned numbers. This information is needed to use such commands as CHANGE QUEUE or KILL QUEUE (see Modules 20 and 49).

## TYPICAL OPERATION

In this activity, you display queue information for printer number 0 (the first printer on the fileserver). Begin at the : prompt of your fileserver.

1. Type **QUEUE 0** and press **Enter**. The screen displays:

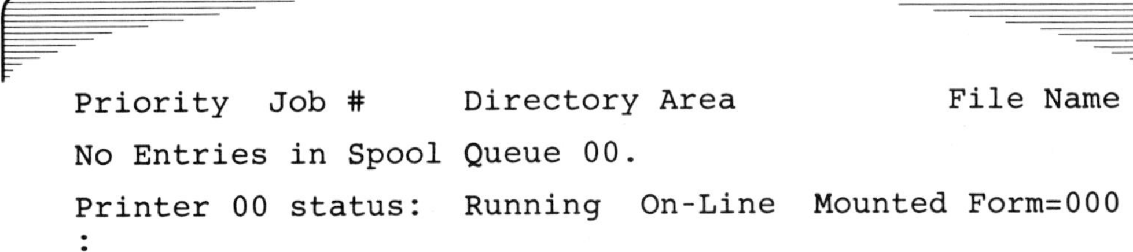

```
Priority  Job #     Directory Area            File Name
No Entries in Spool Queue 00.
Printer 00 status:  Running  On-Line  Mounted Form=000
:
```

2. Turn to Module 20 to continue the learning sequence.

# Module 75

## QUEUE (PUBLIC)

### DESCRIPTION

The public menu-driven utility QUEUE is valid only under NetWare versions 2.0 and below. For versions 2.1 and above use PCONSOLE in Module 67. QUEUE allows you to view the status of network printers, print queues, and print jobs. Print queues hold print jobs produced by NPRINT and SPOOL (Modules 63 and 92). The jobs are sent to the appropriate network printer one at a time. QUEUE also allows users with supervisor privileges to delete print jobs. Do not confuse the command with the console command of the same name (Module 74). QUEUE's menu offers these selections:

**Change Current Printer** This selection provides a list of available fileservers. Use Up Arrow, Down Arrow, and Enter to select the fileserver whose print queues you wish to view. A list of that fileserver's printers is then displayed. Select one.

**Display Print Queue** This selection displays the contents of the currently selected queue. If you have supervisor privileges, you can use Up Arrow, Down Arrow, and Del to delete print jobs. You can also use the Ins key to place files to be printed directly into the queue at whatever position you want. When you press Ins, QUEUE prompts you for the path and a filename to be printed. This has an effect similar to NPRINT.

**Display Printer Information** This selection displays various information about the currently selected printer, including printer number, fileserver to which it is attached, and printer status (On-Line/Off-Line).

### APPLICATIONS

All users can use QUEUE to check the status of print jobs. When a job is no longer shown in a queue, you know it is ready to collect at the network printer. When several network printers are available, use QUEUE to determine which queue has the fewest jobs waiting. Supervisors can also use QUEUE to delete print jobs when it is determined that one is no longer needed. This saves time, as well as printer supplies. Supervisors can also insert print jobs directly into the queue at whatever position they want.

## TYPICAL OPERATION

In this activity, you use QUEUE to display the contents of the queue for printer 0 on the current fileserver. Begin at the DOS prompt of a logged in workstation.

1. Type **QUEUE** and press **Enter**. Notice the following display:

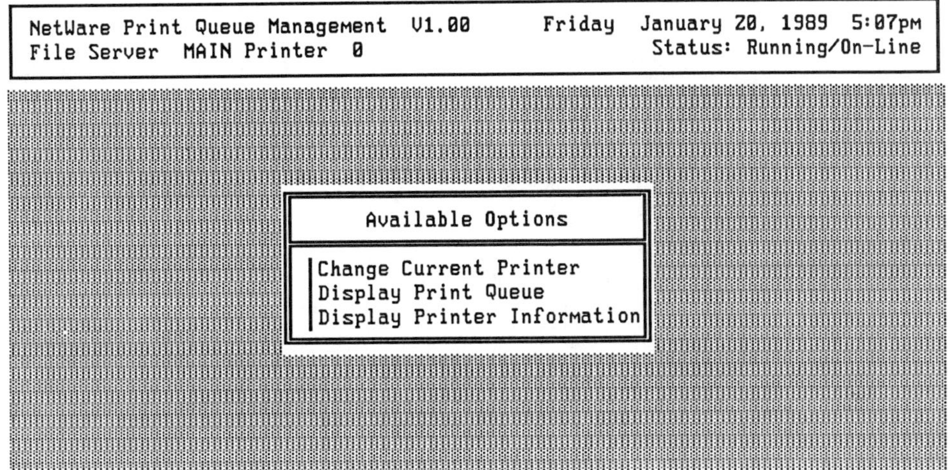


2. Press **Up Arrow** and **Down Arrow** to select Display Print Queue and press **Enter**. The display resembles the following:

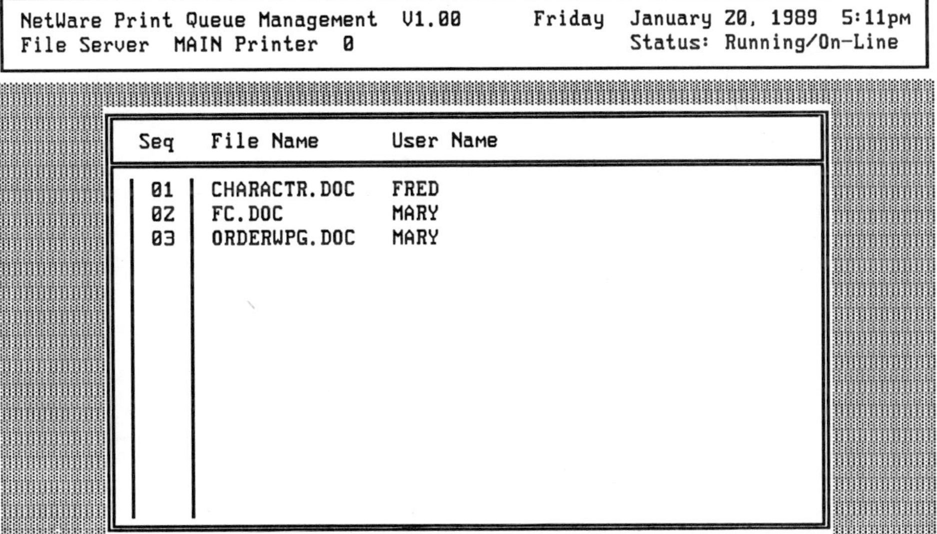

Now view QUEUE's information on printer 0.

3. Press **Esc** to return to the QUEUE main menu.
4. Highlight the selection Display Printer Information and press **Enter**. Your display now shows a screen similar to this:

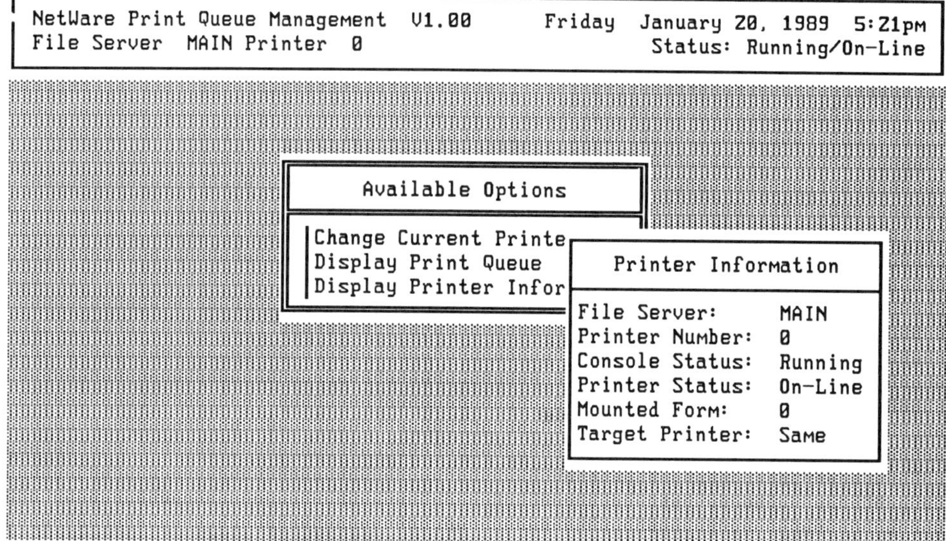


Now exit from QUEUE as follows.

5. Press **Alt-F10**. When the Exit box appears press **Enter** to accept Yes. You are returned to the DOS prompt.
6. Turn to Module 64 to continue the learning sequence.

# Module 76

## REMOVE

### DESCRIPTION

The public command REMOVE is only valid in NetWare versions 2.1 and above. It is used to remove any existing right that a given user or group has within a directory. A user or group which is REMOVEd from a given directory is no longer considered a "trustee" of that directory. The command is followed by the name of the user or group and the directory name. The same action can be accomplished in a menu-driven environment using SYSCON (see Module 95).

### APPLICATIONS

REMOVE provides a quick, easy way to deny users all rights to a given directory. If the information kept in a directory becomes sensitive and requires increased security, existing trustees of that directory can be REMOVEd. Their rights can be later restored using the public command GRANT (see Module 43).

### TYPICAL OPERATION

In this activity, you REMOVE the user GUEST as a trustee of the directory SYS:INN. GUEST is a username created by NetWare at the time of installation. You created SYS:INN in Module 10. Begin at the DOS prompt of a logged in workstation.

1. Type **REMOVE GUEST FROM SYS:INN** and press **Enter**. The word "FROM" is optional. You are returned to a DOS prompt. Verify the removal of GUEST from SYS:INN. Log in as GUEST and change to the \INN directory. Try viewing the files in that directory.
2. Type **LOGIN GUEST** and press **Enter**.
3. Type **CD\INN** and press **Enter**.
4. Type **DIR** and press **Enter**. Your display tells you "File not found."
5. Turn to Module 40 to continue the learning sequence.

# Module 77

## RENDIR

### DESCRIPTION

The public command RENDIR is only valid in NetWare versions 2.1 and above. RENDIR is used to rename a given directory. The command is followed by the old directory name, then the new name with the following syntax: RENDIR *current directory* TO *new name*. The word "TO" is optional. This ability is limited to users who have been assigned "parental" and "modify" rights to the directory which is to be changed. Such rights are assigned using RIGHTS or SYSCON, Modules 81 and 95.

### APPLICATIONS

The naming of directories is important in maintaining a well organized network volume. If a directory name is no longer descriptive of its purpose, or if the creation of a new directory causes conflict with an existing directory name, use RENDIR to change the name. Remember that other users (as well as the LOGIN SCRIPTS, Module 52) may be expecting the old directory name. Be sure to inform users of such changes as appropriate.

### TYPICAL OPERATION

In this activity, you create a subdirectory called SYS:INN \ APPLE, then change the name of the directory to SYS:INN \ ORANGE. The SYS:INN directory was created in Module 10. Begin at the DOS prompt of a logged in workstation.

1. Type **CD \ INN** and press **Enter**. Next type **MD APPLE** and press **Enter**. These are standard DOS commands. To verify the creation of the directory, type **DIR** and press **Enter**. Your display shows:

```
F>DIR
 Volume in drive F is SYS
 Directory of  F:\INN
TEST      TXT       1619   9-05-89   5:15a
APPLE          <DIR>      10-02-89   5:18a
        2 File(s)  36745216 bytes free
F>
```

2. Type **RENDIR SYS:INN \ APPLE TO SYS:INN \ ORANGE** and press **Enter**. The word "TO" is optional. To display the change, once again type **DIR** and press **Enter**. You now see:

```
F>DIR
 Volume in drive F is SYS
 Directory of  F:\INN
TEST      TXT       1619   9-05-89   5:15a
ORANGE         <DIR>      10-02-89   5:19a
        2 File(s)  36745216 bytes free
F>
```

3. Turn to Module 56 to continue the learning sequence.

# Module 78

## REROUTE PRINTER

### DESCRIPTION

The console command REROUTE PRINTER is valid only under NetWare versions 2.0 and below. Under NetWare 2.1 and above use the ADD QUEUE command described in Module 70. REROUTE PRINTER redirects a given print queue to a different printer. The command syntax is:

```
REROUTE PRINTER source destination
```

where *source* and *destination* are fileserver printer numbers 0 through 4. When the command is issued, NetWare issues a STOP PRINTER command (see Module 94) to the source printer, immediately halting output to that printer. Next NetWare transfers that output to the destination printer. Any file that was currently printing on the source printer, any files waiting in its queue, and all files thereafter sent to its queue are now directed to the destination printer. Files sent to the destination printer's queue will continue to print normally. This remains in effect until the source printer is restarted with the START PRINTER command (see Module 93).

### APPLICATIONS

Use REROUTE PRINTER to temporarily stop usage of a given printer without losing or interrupting its queued print jobs. This is useful when a printer must be serviced or temporarily removed from a fileserver. Network users can continue their work as usual.

### TYPICAL OPERATION

This activity requires the presence of at least two printers attached to the fileserver — printers 0 and 1. For an explanation of network printer installation see Module 7. First, you print the file named TEST.TXT (as created in Module 10) to printer 0. Begin at the DOS prompt of a logged in workstation.

1. Type **NPRINT SYS:INN/TEST.TXT P=0** and press **Enter**.

As the file prints, you redirect printer 0 output to printer 1, then resend the file to printer 0.

2. At the fileserver console prompt type **REROUTE PRINTER 0 1** and press **Enter.**
3. At the workstation type **NPRINT SYS:INN/TEST.TXT P=0** and press **Enter.**

Note that the file is rerouted to printer 1. Now return the print queues to their normal state, as follows.

4. At the fileserver console prompt type **START PRINTER 0** and press **Enter.**
5. Turn to Module 80 to continue the learning sequence.

# Module 79

## REVOKE

### DESCRIPTION

The public command REVOKE is only valid in NetWare versions 2.1 and above. You use REVOKE to remove certain rights that a given user (or group) may have for a given directory. It is similar to REMOVE (see Module 76) except that it allows you to REVOKE only the rights you select. These rights are assigned using the public command GRANT (see Module 43). They can also be assigned or revoked in a menu-driven environment using SYSCON (see Module 95). You follow the command by the initials of the rights to be REVOKEd, the directory name, and the user or group name in this format:

```
REVOKE xxx FOR directory name FROM username
```

There are eight basic rights:

| | |
|---|---|
| READ | DELETE |
| WRITE | PARENTAL |
| OPEN | SEARCH |
| CLOSE | MODIFY |

You can also use the keyword ALL to specify all eight rights. Using REVOKE ALL has the same effect as the REMOVE command.

### APPLICATIONS

REVOKE provides a quick, easy way to deny users certain rights to a given directory. If the information kept in a directory becomes sensitive and requires increased security, you may wish to deny some rights of other users. Their rights can be later restored using the public command GRANT (see Module 43).

### TYPICAL OPERATION

In this activity, you REVOKE the user GUEST's right to read files in the SYS:INN directory. GUEST is a username created by NetWare during installation. You created SYS:INN in Module 10. Begin at the DOS prompt on a logged in workstation.

1. Type **REVOKE R FOR \INN FROM GUEST** and press **Enter**. The word "FROM" is optional. You are returned to a DOS prompt.

Verify that the right to read files in the SYS:INN directory has been REVOKEd. Log in as GUEST. Then change to the \INN directory and try to read a file.

2. Type **LOGIN GUEST** and press **Enter.**
3. Type **CD\INN** and press **Enter.**
4. Type **DIR** and press **Enter.** No files will be listed on the screen.
5. Turn to Module 76 to continue the learning sequence.

# Module 80

## REWIND PRINTER

### DESCRIPTION

The console command REWIND PRINTER backs up the specified print queue a given number of pages or to the beginning of the current print job. The command syntax is:

```
REWIND PRINTER printer pages
```

where *printer* is a number 0 through 4, indicating which printer attached to the fileserver is being "rewound," and *pages* is the number of pages to back up. The maximum number of pages you can back up is nine. If you use zero or a number greater than nine, the print job restarts from the beginning.

### APPLICATIONS

The most common use for REWIND PRINTER is to restart a print job that is printing incorrectly. For example, if a job is not lined up correctly, the paper is stuck or torn, or the ribbon needs replacing, take the printer off-line, correct the problem, issue REWIND PRINTER, and put the printer back on-line.

### TYPICAL OPERATION

In this activity, you begin printing the file TEST.TXT (as created in Module 10) on the fileserver's first printer — printer number 0. After interrupting the file while it is being printed, you use the REWIND PRINTER command to back up and start again. Begin at the DOS prompt of a logged in workstation.

1. Type **NPRINT SYS:INN\TEST.TXT P=0** and press **Enter**.
2. Quickly (while the file is printing) take printer 0 off-line by pressing the ONLINE or SELECT button on the printer or by turning it off.
3. Re-align the paper in the printer.

4. At the fileserver console prompt, type **REWIND PRINTER 0 0** and press **Enter**.
5. Put the printer back on-line by pressing the ON LINE or SELECT button or by turning it back on. The print job restarts from the beginning.
6. Turn to Module 41 to continue the learning sequence.

# Module 81

## RIGHTS

### DESCRIPTION

A listing of the rights or privileges that you have been assigned in a given directory is obtained using the public command RIGHTS. This can also be done in a menu-driven environment using the SYSCON utility (see Module 95). To specify a directory, follow the command with a backslash and the complete directory path or its path relative to your current directory. Omit the directory name to view your rights in the current default directory.

These rights may include:

| | |
|---|---|
| READ | View an open file's content |
| WRITE | Add to or change an open file's contents |
| OPEN | Prepare a file for access |
| CREATE | Create a new file |
| DELETE | Completely erase a file |
| PARENTAL | Create subdirectories |
| SEARCH | List files in a directory (like DOS DIR) |
| MODIFY | Change the attributes of a file (see Module 40) |

They are assigned and modified using the SYSCON utility and, in NetWare versions 2.1 and *above*, through GRANT (see Module 43).

### APPLICATIONS

Use RIGHTS to determine what file privileges you have in a given directory.

### TYPICAL OPERATION

In this activity, you list your assigned rights for the current directory. Begin at the DOS prompt on a logged in workstation.

1. Type **RIGHTS** and press **Enter**. The screen should resemble this:

```
F>RIGHTS
SERVER_MAIN/SYS:
Your Directory Rights are [RWOCDPSM]:
    You may Read from Files.                              (R)
    You may Write to Files.                               (W)
    You may Open existing Files.                          (O)
    You may Create new Files.                             (C)
    You may Delete existing Files.                        (D)
    You may change Users' Directory Rights.               (P)
    You may make new Subdirectories.                      (P)
    You may Erase existing Subdirectories.                (P)
    You may Search the Directory.                         (S)
    You may Modify File Status Flags.                     (M)

    You have ALL RIGHTS to this directory area.
F>
```

Now check your rights for a different directory — \PUBLIC.

2. Type **RIGHTS \PUBLIC** and press **Enter**. Note the display:

```
F>RIGHTS \PUBLIC
SERVER_MAIN/SYS:PUBLIC
Your Directory Rights are [RWOCDPSM]:
    You may Read from Files.                              (R)
    You may Write to Files.                               (W)
    You may Open existing Files.                          (O)
    You may Create new Files.                             (C)
    You may Delete existing Files.                        (D)
    You may change Users' Directory Rights.               (P)
    You may make new Subdirectories.                      (P)
    You may Erase existing Subdirectories.                (P)
    You may Search the Directory.                         (S)
    You may Modify File Status Flags.                     (M)

    You have ALL RIGHTS to this directory area.
F>
```

3. Turn to Module 43 to continue the learning sequence.

# Module 82

## SALVAGE

### DESCRIPTION

The public command SALVAGE "un-erases" files which have not yet been permanently deleted. The DOS ERASE (also called DEL) command appears to delete files but they are recoverable using the SALVAGE command. However, once any other file is deleted or created, or the PURGE command is issued (see Module 72), the previously ERASEd file is lost and cannot be SALVAGEd.

The filename(s) to be salvaged can be preceded with a complete path and can include the * and ? wildcard characters. If you do not specify a path or filename, all salvageable files in the default volume are restored.

### APPLICATIONS

Use SALVAGE to restore accidentally ERASEd files.

### TYPICAL OPERATION

In this activity, you ERASE a file named TEST.TXT, then restore it using SALVAGE. Begin at the DOS prompt of a logged in workstation in the SYS:INN directory.

1. Type **ERASE TEST.TXT** and press **Enter**.

**CAUTION**

At this point, if you issue the PURGE command or if you perform any operation that creates, deletes, or erases other files, the TEST.TXT will be permanently lost.

2. Type **SALVAGE TEST.TXT** and press **Enter**. TEST.TXT is now restored to its original condition. Notice the display:

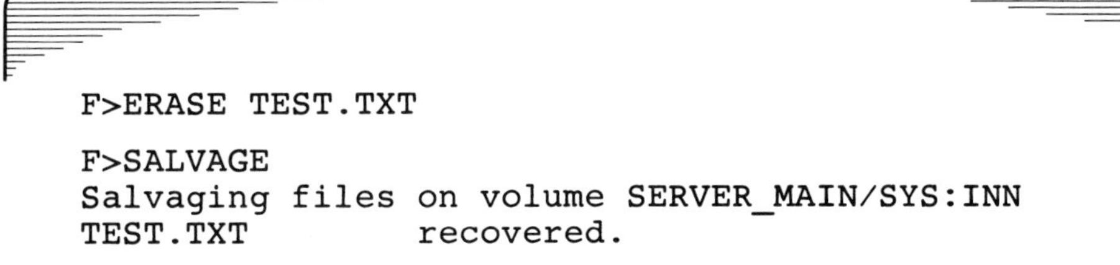

```
F>ERASE TEST.TXT

F>SALVAGE
Salvaging files on volume SERVER_MAIN/SYS:INN
TEST.TXT        recovered.

F>
```

3. Turn to Module 72 to continue the learning sequence.

# Module 83

## SECURITY

### DESCRIPTION

SECURITY is a system command only valid in NetWare versions 2.1 and above. This is a seemingly "intelligent" command that analyzes the network for potential weak points in security. These include:

- Allowing users to have no password, short passwords (less than five characters), or passwords that are the same as the username.
- Allowing users to have rights in the root directory (and thus possible rights in all other directories), or more than the default rights in the \SYSTEM, \PUBLIC, and other NetWare system directories.
- Allowing users to have "supervisor" status, and thus full access to all resources of the network.

SECURITY checks for such occurrences and reports them on your workstation display. You can obtain a hard copy of the SECURITY findings by using the DOS "> PRN" to redirect screen output to a printer.

### APPLICATIONS

NetWare is capable of very sophisticated security configurations, but there are a number of oversights an administrator may make in maintaining the system. Therefore, it is important to periodically run SECURITY and correct any reported problems as you see fit.

### TYPICAL OPERATION

In this activity, you print a report of potential network security breaks. Begin at the DOS prompt of a logged in workstation.

1. To send the report to a local printer, first ensure that the local printer port is not redirected to the network—type **ENDCAP** and press **Enter**.

2. To direct the report to a network printer (in this case printer 0 on the default server), type **CAPTURE L = 0 P = 0** and press **Enter**. ENDCAP and CAPTURE are covered in Modules 34 and 17.
3. Type **SECURITY > PRN** and press **Enter**.
4. Turn to Module 14 to continue the learning sequence.

# Module 84

## SEND (CONSOLE)

### DESCRIPTION

The console command SEND transmits a given message to all specified workstations. It is similar to BROADCAST (see Module 16). You follow SEND by a message of up to 40 characters, enclosed in quotation marks and then a list of workstation numbers, separated by commas. Omission of the list causes the message to be sent to everyone. To clear the message press Ctrl-Enter.

### APPLICATIONS

Use SEND in place of BROADCAST when sending messages to specific workstations.

### TYPICAL OPERATION

In this activity, you send the message "PRINTER 0 IS BROKEN!" to the users on workstations 1 and 2. Begin at the : prompt of your fileserver.

1. Type **SEND "PRINTER 0 IS BROKEN" TO 1,2** and press **Enter**.

The message appears on line 25 of workstations 1 and 2 and also at the bottom of the fileserver console. (See Module 22 to clear the message from the console.)

2. Turn to Module 22 to continue the learning sequence.

# Module 85

## SEND (PUBLIC)

### DESCRIPTION

The public command SEND transmits messages immediately to other users. The messages can be from one to 40 characters and must always be enclosed in quotes. The message is displayed on the 25th (bottom) line of the designated user's screen. The menu-driven utility SESSION (Module 86) also allows the sending of messages.

You can specify one or more users to receive a single message, or use the group name EVERYONE. Versions of NetWare 2.1 and above also allow any other existing group name. If the recipient is not logged in to the default file server, you must precede their username by their fileserver name and a forward slash. You can use a wildcard (*) to represent all fileservers to which you are attached. If you attempt to SEND a message to a non-existent user or one who has not logged in, you receive an appropriate message concerning that situation. A user's current station number can be substituted for a username. A list of logged in users and their current station numbers can be obtained via the USERLIST command. Finally, *console* can be specified as a username to send messages to fileservers.

To clear a message which you receive, press Ctrl-Enter.

### APPLICATIONS

SEND is a very useful command and should ideally be learned by all users. It can greatly enhance inter-office communication, as well as streamline the job of the network administrator.

### TYPICAL OPERATION

In this activity, you use the SEND command to transmit several messages. The first message is to a user named Fred who is logged in to the ACCT fileserver. Begin at the DOS prompt of a logged in workstation.

1. Type **SEND "Have the income statement finished by noon" to ACCT/FRED** and press **Enter**. Your screen resembles this:

```
F>SEND "Have the income statement finished by noon" to ACCT/FRED
Message sent to SERVER_MAIN/FRED (station 1).

F>
```

In the following step, you SEND a message to both Bob and Fred. They are logged in to the default fileserver.

2. Type **SEND "Come to my office at once!" to FRED, BOB** and press **Enter.**

Next, SEND a message to everyone on the default fileserver.

3. Type **SEND "Log out by 5:00" to EVERYONE** and press **Enter.**

SEND the next message to all users on all attached fileservers.

4. Type **SEND "Log out by 5:00" to */EVERYONE** and press **Enter.**

Finally, SEND a message to the fileserver.

5. Type **SEND "Change printer 1 to font cartridge B" to CONSOLE** and press **Enter.**
6. Turn to Module 18 to continue the learning sequence.

# Module 86

## SESSION

### DESCRIPTION

SESSION is a menu-driven utility used to interface with NetWare without causing any changes to the network environment that last beyond the current session. In other words, any configuration changes made with SESSION are temporary and cease to exist after logging out. Therefore, SESSION is a suitable utility for all users. SESSION includes the following options:

**Change Current Server** This lists available fileservers and allows you to select the one which will be your default.

**Drive Mappings** This allows you to view and change the current drive mappings (see MAP, Module 56).

**Group List** This lists all groups and allows you to send a message to any select group.

**Search Mappings** This allows you to view and change search mappings (once again, refer to MAP, Module 56).

**Select Default Drive** This lets you determine which drive will be your current default drive.

**User List** This is similar to the public command USERLIST (Module 100). It provides a list of all current users. You can select any user and view information concerning them, or send them a message.

As with all menu-driven utilities, use the Up and Down Arrow keys to make your selections. The Esc key moves you back through the menus. Press Alt-F10 and Y to exit.

### APPLICATIONS

SESSION allows users to change drive mappings, select default drives, attach to fileservers, and send messages, all from within a user-friendly menu-driven environment. Many users may not want to learn and remember such commands as MAP, ATTACH, and SEND. They will find it easier to use SESSION.

## TYPICAL OPERATION

In this activity, you use two of the options available within SESSION. Begin at the DOS prompt of a logged in workstation.

1. Type **SESSION** and press **Enter**. The screen resembles this:

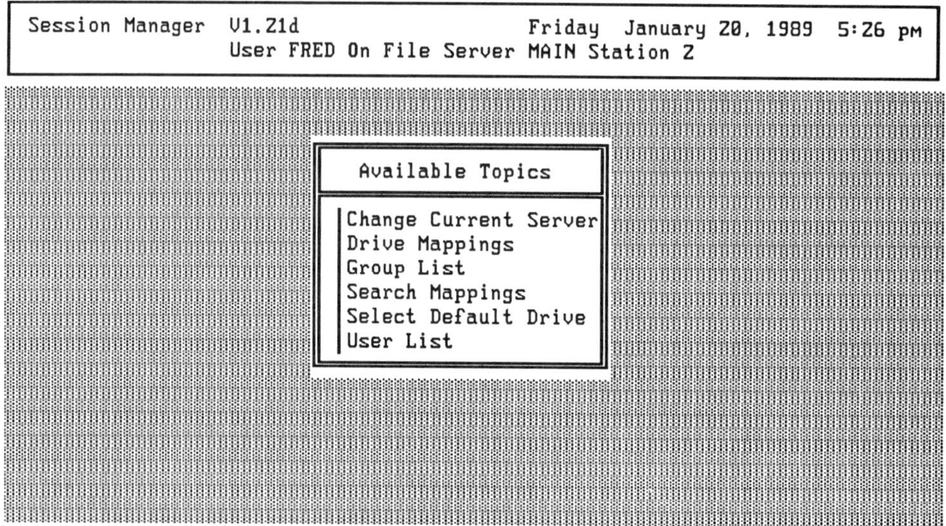


2. Press **Enter** to select the first option, Change Current Server. By selecting this option, you are actually performing the public command ATTACH. Since it is assumed that you only have one fileserver to which you may be attached, only the name of your fileserver will be shown in the box, as is shown here:

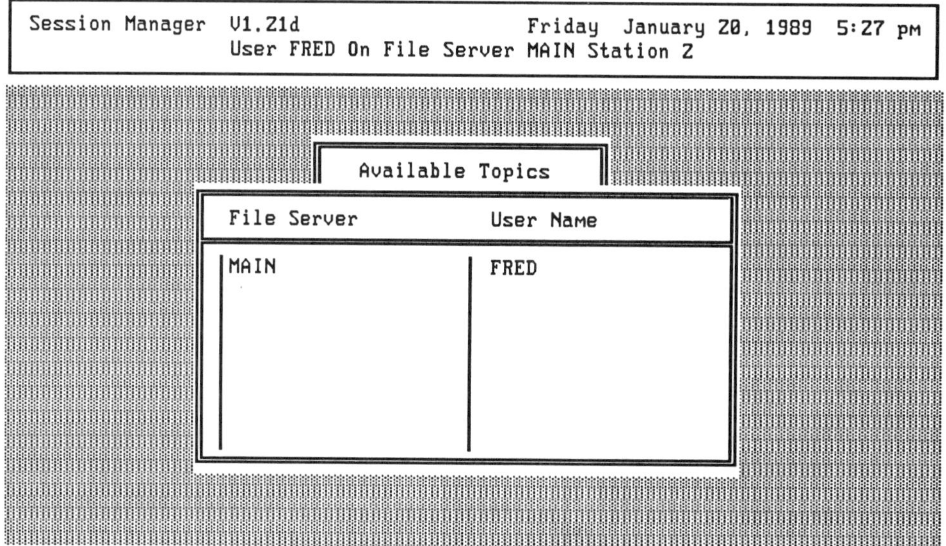

3. Press **Esc** to back up to the Available Topics menu.
4. Press **Down Arrow** to select User List and press **Enter**. This selection is the same as typing USERLIST at the workstation's DOS prompt. The screen resembles the following:

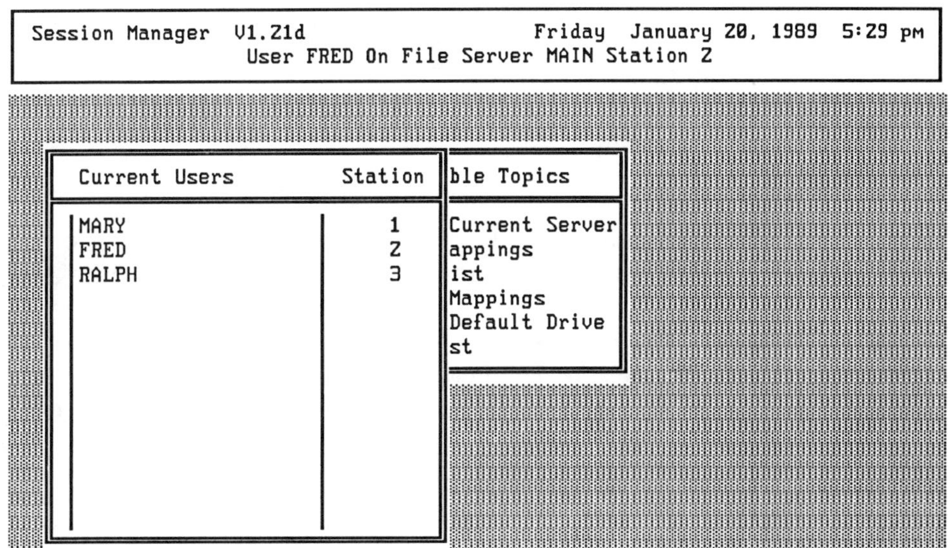


5. Press **Esc** to again backup to the Available Topics menu.
6. Press **Alt-F10** to exit SESSION. Highlight "Yes" and press **Enter**.
7. Turn to Module 39 to continue the learning sequence.

# Module 87

## SET TIME

### DESCRIPTION

You use the console command SET TIME to change the fileserver's clock to the actual date and time. You follow the command by the correct date and/or time, separated by a space. It is not necessary to specify both the time and date if one of them is already correct. Enter the time in the form HOUR:MINUTE:SECOND. Seconds can be omitted. The hour is a number 0—12, 10:30 A.M. is entered 10:30:00AM; and 10:30 P.M. is entered 22:30:00PM. If A.M. and P.M. are omitted, NetWare assumes hours, with 8:00—11:59 being A.M. and 12:00—6:00 being P.M. Enter the date as MM/DD/YY.

### APPLICATIONS

Use SET TIME to correct an invalid date and/or time when a fileserver is booted (see Module 10). If the fileserver is always left on or has a battery powered clock, the date and time should be automatically maintained (even in leap years). Daylight savings time, however, is not accounted for and will require adjusting the time with SET TIME.

### TYPICAL OPERATION

In this activity, you change the fileserver's date and time to 01/12/89 and 15:15:00 (3:15 P.M.) then change it back to the current date and time. Begin at the : prompt of your fileserver.

1. Type **SET TIME 01/12/89 15:15:00** and press **Enter**.

Now, use the TIME command (see Module 97) to verify that the change has occurred.

2. Type **TIME** and press **Enter**. The display will show the time that you entered in step 1.
3. Type **SET TIME** followed by today's date and the correct time and press **Enter**. Be sure to use the TIME command to verify the correct time and date.
4. Turn to Module 25 to continue the learning sequence.

# Module 88

## SETPASS

### DESCRIPTION

SETPASS is a public command which allows you to assign or exchange the password associated with your username. This can also be accomplished in a menu-driven environment using the SYSCON utility (see Module 95). To change your password on a fileserver other than the default, you can follow the SETPASS command with a valid fileserver name. Passwords are up to 15 characters in length in versions 2.0 and below or 127 characters in versions 2.1 and above and can combine alpha and numeric characters. They cannot include control characters.

### APPLICATIONS

To quickly create or change your password, use SETPASS.

### TYPICAL OPERATION

In this activity, you assign the password "SUNSHINE" to your username on the current default fileserver. Begin at the DOS prompt.

1. Type **SETPASS** and press **Enter**. Note the display:

```
F>SETPASS
Enter your old password:
```

2. Type your old password and press **Enter**. If you are assigning your password for the first time, press **Enter**. The screen responds:

```
Enter your new password:
```

3. Type **SUNSHINE** and press **Enter**. The characters are not displayed as you type them. NetWare does not distinguish between uppercase and lowercase. You are now asked to verify:

```
Retype your new password:
```

4. Once more, type **SUNSHINE** and press **Enter**. Be careful to remember your new password. In versions 2.0 and below the supervisor can retrieve your password using SYSCON if you forget it. Note the display:

```
Your password has been changed.
F>
```

5. Turn to Module 102 to continue the learning sequence.

# Module 89

## SHOWFILE

### DESCRIPTION

SHOWFILE is a system command which cancels the effects of HIDEFILE (see Module 45). SHOWFILE restores the ability to list specified files and to delete or copy over them.

You follow the command with the name of the file to show. You can precede the filename with its path (drive specification and directory name) if different from the current path. You can also use wildcards (* and ?) in specifying the filename(s).

### APPLICATIONS

To make files which were previously hidden and protected by HIDEFILE available to all users, use SHOWFILE.

### TYPICAL OPERATION

In this activity, you remove the hidden and protected status of a file named TEST.TXT which was hidden in Module 45. Begin at the DOS prompt of a logged in workstation in the SYS:INN directory.

1. Type **SHOWFILE TEST.TXT** and press **Enter**. The screen resembles this:

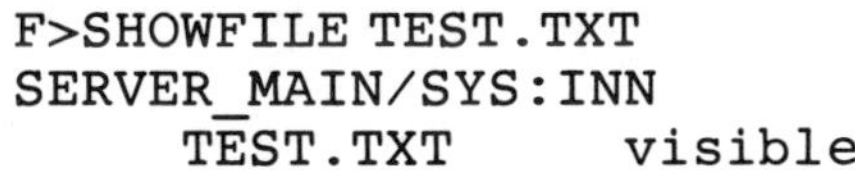

```
F>SHOWFILE TEST.TXT
SERVER_MAIN/SYS:INN
     TEST.TXT     visible

F>
```

2. Turn to Module 38 to continue the learning sequence.

# Module 90

## SLIST

### DESCRIPTION

The public command SLIST lists all active fileservers attached to your default server. Fileservers which are not currently on-line are not listed. Included in the fileserver listing is the name of the network on which each fileserver resides, as well as the node address (a unique hexadecimal number assigned to each NIC). On single fileserver networks the SLIST command is of little importance.

### APPLICATIONS

On a network with more than one server, use SLIST to determine what fileservers are available to you.

### TYPICAL OPERATION

In this activity, you list all operational fileservers physically attached to your default server. Begin at the DOS prompt of a logged in workstation.

1. Type **SLIST** and press **Enter**. A list of known servers and the node addresses is displayed:

```
F>SLIST

Known NetWare File Servers    Network     Node Address
--------------------------    --------    ------------
SERVER_MAIN                   [      1] [          FE]
                                                (Default)

Total of 1 File Servers.

F>
```

2. Turn to Module 13 to continue the learning sequence.

# Module 91
## SMODE

**DESCRIPTION**

The public command SMODE is valid only in NetWare versions 2.1 and above. SMODE determines the way in which specified executable files will search for data files. Most applications require access to data files. Under DOS, data files are either located in the same directory as the application, or the application is written to look for data in other specific directories. NetWare can limit these two options or provide the application the ability to search for data stored in other directories. These alternate search directories are established using the MAP command, either as a public command (see Module 56) or in LOGIN SCRIPTS (see Module 52). There are six ways to search:

| | |
|---|---|
| 0 | This is the default. It tells NetWare to follow search modes established in the SHELL.CFG file (see Module 8). |
| 1 | In this mode, applications will search *only* in directories as determined in the program. If none are specified in the program, NetWare will search the current default directory and, finally, the search paths defined by MAP. |
| 2 | In this mode, the application only searches the current default directory. |
| 3 | This mode is the same as mode 1, except that any directories not specified in the program can only be opened "read-only." |
| 5 | This mode is like mode 1, except that if the needed data files are not found in the directory specified in the program, NetWare continues its search—first in the default directory, then in the search paths defined by MAP. |
| 7 | In this mode, applications may search directories specified in the program, the default directory, and the search paths, as long as the data files are opened "read-only." |

Modes 4 and 6 are currently not defined.

The SMODE command is followed by the path (if different than the current default) and the filename of the program, then the mode number. The typical syntax is:

SMODE *fileserver name/volume name:directory name\filemask mode*

If any of the information is omitted, the default is assumed. If a mode is not specified, the current SMODE status is displayed.

## APPLICATIONS

SMODE is used both to expand and to limit the way in which applications search for data. You may have an application whose data you wish to keep in different directories. If the application does not allow you to tell it where to look for data files, mode 5 will allow it any search paths established by the MAP command. On the other hand, it is possible that different applications may use data files of the same name. It is important that your program not read the files of others. Use mode 2 to limit access to data files in the current default directory.

## TYPICAL OPERATION

In this activity, you restrict a hypothetical program named 321.EXE located in a directory called SYS:INN from accessing data files located outside that directory. Begin at the DOS prompt of a logged in workstation.

1. Type **SMODE SYS:INN\321.EXE 2** and press **Enter**. The display shows:

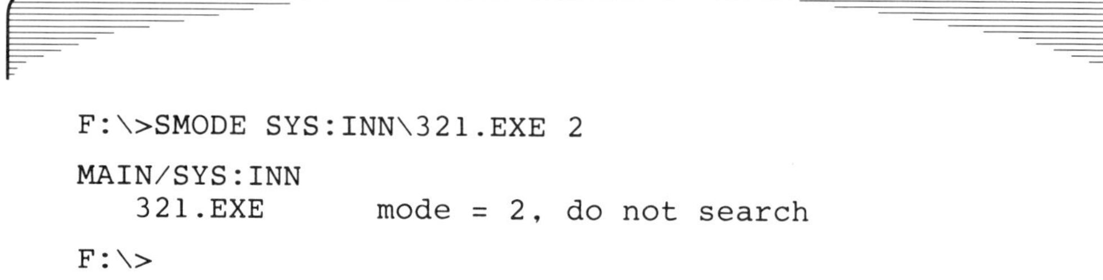

```
F:\>SMODE SYS:INN\321.EXE 2

MAIN/SYS:INN
   321.EXE      mode = 2, do not search

F:\>
```

2. Turn to Module 61 to continue the learning sequence.

# Module 92

## SPOOL

### DESCRIPTION

SPOOL is only valid in NetWare versions 2.0 and before. Later versions use a very similar command called CAPTURE (see Module 17). SPOOL is a public command which redirects subsequent printer output to a spool file which is then transferred to the appropriate print queue.

Under DOS 2.x, the output is accumulated until you issue the ENDSPOOL command. DOS 3.x automatically sends the spooled output to the print queue when you exit the application. Either way, the spool file is automatically deleted after being sent to the queue. There are 16 flags that affect the way in which spooled output is printed. Many of them are similar to the flags used with NPRINT (see Module 63). You can use the full name or the abbreviation of each one. (If you do not use flags, the defaults mentioned in the following descriptions are used.)

**B =** **(Banner = )** The parameter is text, which can be up to twelve characters and is printed on the banner page preceding the printout. The default is LST:.

**C =** **(Copies = )** The parameter is the number of copies to print. The allowed range is 0 to 255. The default is 1.

**CR =** **(Create = )** The parameter is a filename which can be preceded with a full path. When you use this flag, output is saved to the given filename, as well as to the spool file. Thus, after the spool file is printed, additional printouts can be obtained by NPRINTing the CREATEd file. The default is to not create an output file.

**NOTE**

If a fileserver is specified in the path of the filename to be CREATEd, it overrides any fileserver name specified with the S flag. The SPOOLed output is sent to the selected printer number attached to the fileserver indicated by the CREATE flag.

D (**Disable**) There are no parameters. This flag disables any default values for the SPOOL command. The default is to not disable.

E (**Enable**) There are no parameters. This flag restores SPOOL defaults. It counteracts the DISABLE flag if it was used on a previous SPOOL command. The default is to enable.

F = (**Forms = )** The parameter is a number which specifies the type of form on which the file should be printed. The allowed range is 0 to 255. Just before printing the file, the fileserver to which the target printer is attached verifies that the requested form number is the same as the last one used on that printer. If not, a message is displayed asking that the appropriate form type be loaded. Once an operator has loaded the correct form, printing is resumed by typing START PRINTER at the fileserver console and pressing Enter.

The assignment of form type to form numbers is arbitrary. A list of available forms and their corresponding numbers should be established and provided to all users.

FF (**Form Feed**) There are no parameters. This flag restores automatic form feeds. It counteracts the NFF flag if it was used on a previous SPOOL command. The default is to form feed.

L = (**Local = )** The parameter is a single-digit number indicating the local parallel printer port (LPT1: through LPT3:) which is to be redirected by the SPOOL command. The range is 1 to 3. The default is 1.

NB (**No Banner**) There are no parameters. Include this flag to suppress the printing of a banner page before the file is printed. The default is to print banner pages.

**NFF** **(No Form Feed)** There are no parameters. If the file being printed contains form feed commands, include this command to suppress additional automatic form feeds. The default is automatic form feeds.

**NT** **(No Tabs)** There are no parameters. This flag causes tab characters to be ignored when printing the SPOOLed file. The default is to not ignore tabs.

**P =** **(Printer = )** The parameter indicates which printer on the indicated fileserver is the target for the files to be printed. The printer numbers are defined and can be modified with the INSTALL program (see Module 6). The range is 0 to 5 but is limited, of course, by the number of printers attached to the given fileserver. Remember, the first printer defined on a fileserver is called number 0 and is the default.

**S =** **(Server = )** The parameter is a text string naming any fileserver. This server is the target for the files to be printed. If the server has more than one printer attached, you can select one with the P flag or allow the default of 0. The server chosen does not have to be one to which you are currently logged in or attached. NetWare will temporarily log in to that server, print the files, and log back out. This procedure uses the GUEST username. If a password has been assigned to GUEST, you are prompted to enter it. If the GUEST username has been deleted, you are given the opportunity to log in using any other valid username. The default is the fileserver to which you are currently logged.

**SH** **(Show)** There are no parameters. This flag causes the SPOOL command to list how flag values are currently set. Use it only with no other flags. The default is to not show.

**T =** **(Tabs = )** The parameter is the number of columns which separate the tabs in the files to be printed. The range is 0 to 18. If a file is generated by an application which does not format tabs prior to printing, this flag tells NetWare how to interpret the file. The default is 8.

**TI =** **(Timeout = )** The parameter is a number of seconds to wait after output to the spool file has ceased before issuing an automatic ENDSPOOL. The range is 0 to 1000. Without this flag or with a value of 0, you must exit an application every time you wish spooled output to be printed. As this can be quite an inconvenience, use this flag with a value of 10 or 15 seconds to cause timely automatic printouts. Setting the value to 0 seconds disables automatic ENDSPOOLs. The default is no timeouts (equivalent to TI = 0).

## APPLICATIONS

Some software applications are designed with the ability to send output directly to network printers. When using other programs, issuing the SPOOL command prior to entering the application can allow the easy transfer of output to any printer attached to any available fileserver.

## TYPICAL OPERATION

In this activity, you redirect printouts from LPT2: on your workstation to printer 3 on the default fileserver. Begin at the DOS prompt of a logged in workstation.

1. Type **SPOOL L=2 P=3** and press **Enter**.
2. Now enter any application and produce printouts as you normally would, directing them to LPT2:. They are stored in a temporary spool file. The screen should resemble the following:

```
F>SPOOL L=2 P=3
Device LPT2: re-routed to printer 3 on server SERVER_MAIN.
F>
```

3. Exit the application, type **ENDSPOOL**, and press **Enter**. The output from your application now begins to print on the selected network printer.

```
F>ENDSPOOL
Device LST: set to local mode.
F>
```

Next, use the TI flag to allow immediate printouts while in the application. Also produce two copies of the output.

4. Type **SPOOL TI=15 C=2** and press **Enter**. Notice the display:

```
F>SPOOL TI=15 C=2
Device LPT2: re-routed to printer 2 on server SERVER_MAIN.
F>
```

The L and P flags remain set as in step 1 until they are specifically reset in a SPOOL command.

5. Re-enter your application and produce a printout. This time the printing begins 15 seconds later.
6. Exit your application.
7. Turn to Module 74 to continue the learning sequence.

# Module 93

## START PRINTER

### DESCRIPTION

The console command START PRINTER is only valid under NetWare versions 2.0 and below. Versions 2.1 and above use the ADD QUEUE command (see Module 70). START PRINTER is used to restart a printer where print queue output has been halted by STOP PRINTER, KILL PRINTER, or REROUTE PRINTER (Modules 94, 48, and 78, respectively). You follow the command with the number of the printer (0-4) to be restarted. When the command is issued, any files which are accumulated in the printer's queue will begin printing.

### APPLICATIONS

Use START PRINTER to resume normal printing after the operation for which you STOPPED, KILLED, or REROUTED the printer has been completed.

### TYPICAL OPERATION

In this activity, you restart the printer you STOPPED in Module 94. Begin at the : prompt of your fileserver.

1. Type **START PRINTER 0** and press **Enter**.

The print job sent in Module 41 now begins to print.

2. Turn to Module 49 to continue the learning sequence.

# Module 94

## STOP PRINTER

### DESCRIPTION

The console command STOP PRINTER is only valid under NetWare versions 2.0 and below. Under NetWare versions 2.1 and above use the QUEUE DELETE command (see Module 70). STOP PRINTER halts a printer's queue from sending any additional print jobs to a specified printer. You follow the command by the number of the printer to stop. If a job is currently printing, it is stopped immediately — the printer stops when its internal buffer (if any) is emptied. The jobs still in the queue, along with any additional jobs that are sent while the printer is stopped, are held until the printer is restarted using START PRINTER (Module 93).

### APPLICATIONS

Use STOP PRINTER to temporarily halt the flow of print jobs to the specified printer. This can allow for printer maintenance, such as loading additional paper or ribbons or printer repairs. If the printer is in the middle of a job when stopped, that job can be reprinted from the beginning by using REWIND PRINTER (see Module 80) before restarting the printer.

### TYPICAL OPERATION

In this activity, you stop printer number 0 on the fileserver, then attempt to print the file named TEST.TXT (as created in Module 10). Begin at the : prompt of your fileserver.

1. Type **STOP PRINTER 0** and press **Enter.**
2. At a logged in workstation, type **NPRINT TEST.TXT P = 0** and press **Enter.**

The print job is held in the queue and not sent to the printer. You will restart the printer in the Typical Operation in Module 93.

3. Turn to Module 93 to continue the learning sequence.

# Module 95

## SYSCON

### DESCRIPTION

SYSCON is a menu utility you use to establish, monitor, and alter system configuration information in a number of different ways. This includes fileserver, group, user, and login script information. The SYSCON menu looks like this:

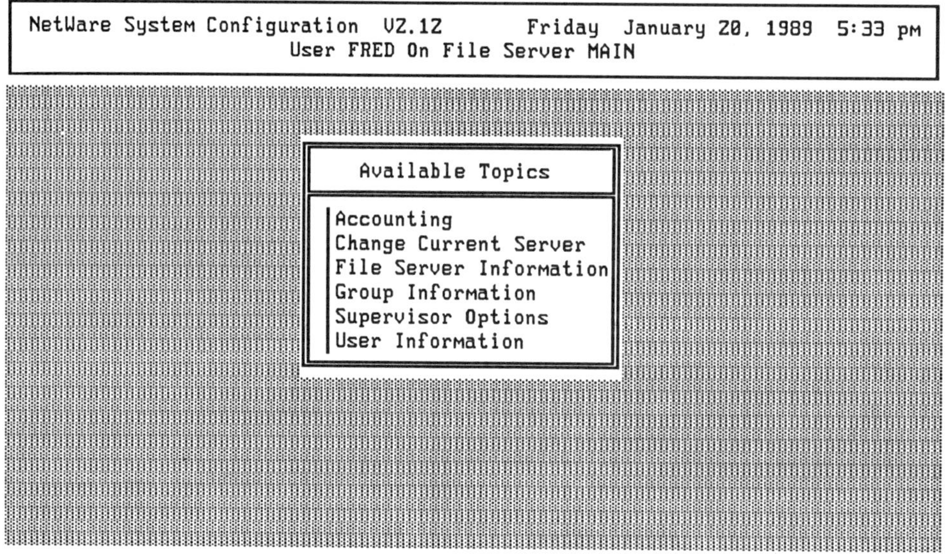


Certain menu selections are available only to users with supervisor privileges. NetWare versions 2.1 and above have several new features in the SYSCON utility, as designated in the following list by the 2.1 in parentheses. The options from the opening menu of SYSCON and their purpose are as follows.

| *Menu Selection* | *Purpose* |
|---|---|
| Accounting (2.1) | Track use of the network by each user to determine use patterns and billing levels. |
| Change Current Server | Select a different fileserver to be configured by SYSCON. |

| | |
|---|---|
| File Server Information | Various information about the type and configuration of fileservers. |
| Group Information | Create, define, and display user groups. |
| System Login Script (2.1) | Define the system login script. In 2.1 and above this option is found under Supervisor Options. |
| Supervisor Options (2.1) | Monitor accounting and login restrictions, define autoexec and login script files, list fileserver errors. |
| User Information | Create, define, and display user information (rights, restrictions, passwords, etc.). |

## APPLICATIONS

While the SYSCON utility is often used by all users on a network, it is most extensively used by network administrators. On newly installed networks, SYSCON allows you to define users and user groups. This includes establishing which files and directories can be accessed by each user or group of users and in what way they can be affected. You can also establish the days and times during which given users can login, passwords for each user, and other security-related information.

Login scripts are defined with the SYSCON utility. These are a set of instructions executed each time a user logs in to a fileserver. The instructions establish drive mappings, search paths, the location of the DOS command processor (COMMAND.COM), and other important information. When a user logs in, an individual login script is executed (if one exists), followed by a system login script (if any) that applies to all users.

SYSCON also allows you to create and maintain a network accounting system. Network accounting tracks use of the fileserver(s) by each user based on time logged in and out, number of requests, amount of data written and read, printer access, and amount of disk storage used. This information is then used to determine a scheme to bill individual users or departments within a company for overall network use.

## TYPICAL OPERATION

In this activity, you use SYSCON to view information about the fileserver. Begin at the DOS prompt of a logged in workstation.

1. Type **SYSCON** and press **Enter**.
2. Highlight File Server Information using the arrow keys and press **Enter**.

A list of available fileservers is displayed. On single server networks, of course, there is only one choice.

3. Highlight one of the fileservers listed and press **Enter**. Your screen now resembles this:

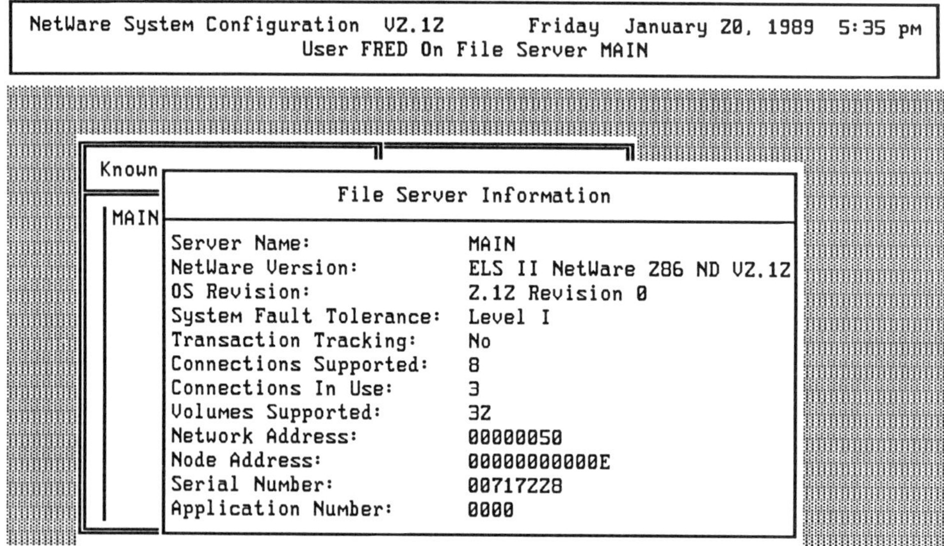


4. Press **Alt-F10** to exit SYSCON. The Exit Syscon box appears.
5. Press **Enter** to accept Yes. You are returned to the DOS prompt.
6. Turn to Module 55 to continue the learning sequence.

# Module 96

## SYSTIME

### DESCRIPTION

The public command SYSTIME displays the current time and date of the fileserver and sets your workstation accordingly. You can include a fileserver name or view the time of the default server by omitting the name.

### APPLICATIONS

Like DOS, NetWare keeps track of the date and time of the last update to each file. It is important for each workstation's internal clock to match the fileserver's. Otherwise this date/time stamping scheme can become erroneous and, therefore, of no use.

### TYPICAL OPERATION

In this activity, you check the time and date of the default fileserver. Begin at the DOS prompt of a logged in workstation.

1. Type **SYSTIME** and press **Enter**. Your display shows a time and date such as:

```
F>SYSTIME
Current System Time:  Thursday, January 12 1989   7:52 pm

F>
```

2. Turn to Module 101 to continue the learning sequence.

# Module 97

## TIME

### DESCRIPTION

The console command TIME displays the fileserver's current date and time. This is maintained by the fileserver as long as it is running. Some fileservers (IBM PC-AT and compatibles) also maintain the current date and time while turned off.

### APPLICATIONS

Use TIME to verify that the correct date and time are set on the fileserver. If incorrect, they can be changed with SET TIME (see Module 87).

### TYPICAL OPERATION

In this activity, you display the current date and time according to the fileserver's internal clock. Begin at the : prompt of your fileserver.

1. Type **TIME** and press **Enter**. You see a display similar to the following:

2. Turn to Module 87 to continue the learning sequence.

# Module 98

## TLIST

### DESCRIPTION

TLIST is a public command valid only in NetWare versions 2.1 and above. It lists the current trustees of given directories and their rights. Trustee rights are assigned using GRANT (see Module 43) or SYSCON (see Module 95). There are eight possible rights:

| | |
|---|---|
| READ | DELETE |
| WRITE | PARENTAL |
| OPEN | SEARCH |
| CLOSE | MODIFY |

*Trustees* are users or groups who have been granted any rights in a given directory. Follow the TLIST command by a directory name then, optionally, a keyword. The keyword "USERS" lists only users; "GROUPS" lists only groups. If neither is used, all trustees are listed.

### APPLICATIONS

It is vital to network security to keep track of which users (or groups) have various rights within different directories. TLIST gives quick access to this information. Used in conjunction with GRANT, REMOVE, and REVOKE (see Modules 43, 76, and 79), TLIST provides command line management of trustee rights.

### TYPICAL OPERATION

In this activity, you list all users' rights in directory SYS:INN (created in Module 10). Begin at the DOS prompt of a logged in workstation.

1. Type **TLIST SYS:INN USERS**. Your display shows something like:

```
F> TLIST SYS:INN USERS
User Trustees:
     FRED       [RWOCDPSM]  (Fred Smith)
     GUEST      [R O     ]  ()
F>
```

2. Turn to Module 79 to continue the learning sequence.

# Module 99

## UDIR

### DESCRIPTION

UDIR is only valid in NetWare versions 2.0 and before. Later versions use a more versatile command called NDIR (see Module 62). UDIR is a public command which lists files that meet given criteria. Use the command by itself to list all files in both the current directory and its subdirectories. The list includes the filename, the size (in bytes), and the date and time the file was last modified. Follow the command with a partial or complete path to get a selective list of files. This path can include fileservers and volumes other than the current default, as well as the * and ? wildcard characters. The typical syntax for this command is:

```
UDIR servername/volume name:directory name\filemask
```

Each of the specifications that follow UDIR are optional. If omitted, the current default is assumed.

### APPLICATIONS

Use UDIR to locate files, determine their size, and find out when they were last changed. UDIR is preferred to the DOS command DIR because it will include subdirectories in the search process. Also, it can be used on drives located on fileservers other than the current default. By using UDIR from the root directory of a volume, you can list any and all directories which contain a file with a given filename.

### TYPICAL OPERATION

In this activity, you search for and list a file named SEND.COM in the SYS:PUBLIC directory. This is one of the command files placed there by NetWare at the time of installation. Then you use the * wildcard character to list all files in this directory with filenames starting with "S." Begin at the DOS prompt of a logged in workstation.

1. Type **UDIR SYS:PUBLIC SEND.COM** and press **Enter**. The screen looks similar to this:

```
F>UDIR SYS:PUBLIC SEND.COM
SERVER_MAIN/SYS:PUBLIC
    SEND      COM        23584   1-30-86    4:53 pm

F>
```

2. Now type **UDIR SYS:PUBLIC S*.*** and press **Enter**. The screen now displays:

```
F>UDIR SYS:PUBLIC S*.*
SERVER_MAIN/SYS:PUBLIC
    SETPASS   EXE        19658   5-20-85    2:44 pm
    SYSCON    EXE       120320   5-15-86    3:53 pm
    SYSCON    HLP        51059   3-07-86   12:34 pm
    SESSION   EXE        90112   3-06-86   11:43 am
    SHOWDIR   COM        21232   2-26-86   11:06 pm
    SALVAGE   EXE        29370   1-15-86   11:09 am
    SEND      COM        23584   1-30-86    4:53 pm
    SLIST     EXE        12423   5-27-87    3:25 pm
    SPOOL     COM        20176   3-07-86    3:23 pm
    SESSION   HLP        17582   1-27-86    8:39 am
    SYS$MSG   DAT        14225   5-02-86   10:36 am
    SYSTIME   EXE        19674   1-15-86   11:08 am

F>
```

3. Turn to Module 50 to continue the learning sequence.

# Module 100
## USERLIST

### DESCRIPTION

USERLIST is a public command used to list the current users on given fileservers. The list of users includes their connection number and when they logged in. Use this command alone for a list of users on the current default fileserver. Or, you can specify fileservers following the command, as well as specific usernames. The NetWare convention of

*FILESERVER NAME/USERNAME*

applies and the DOS wildcards of "*" and "?" can be used.

### APPLICATIONS

Use USERLIST to determine which users are currently logged in to the network or to specific fileservers. This command is commonly used prior to SEND (see Module 84) to determine what users are available to receive messages.

### TYPICAL OPERATION

In this activity, you display a list of all users on the network. Then, you list only users whose usernames start with F. Begin at the DOS prompt of a logged in workstation.

1. Type **USERLIST** and press **Enter**. The screen resembles this:

```
F>USERLIST

User Information for Server SERVER_MAIN
Connection  User Name       Login Time
----------  --------------  ------------------
     1      SUPERVISOR       1/12/89  7:46 pm.
     2      BOB              1/12/89  6:29 am.
     3    * FRED             1/12/89  7:46 pm.

F>
```

Note the "*" on the screen. This signifies who you are logged in as.

2. Type **USERLIST */F*** and press **Enter**. The screen resembles this:

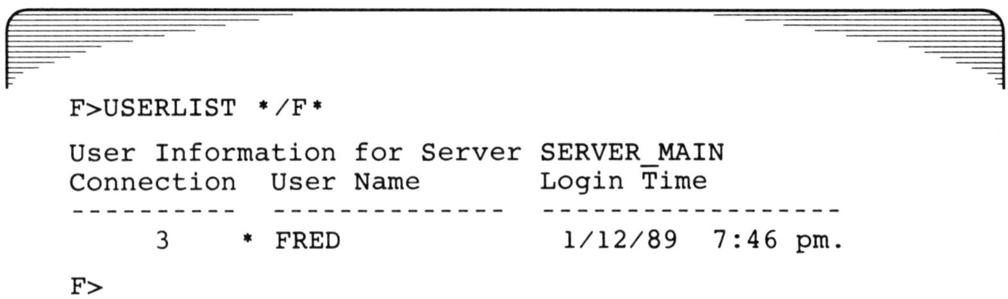

```
F>USERLIST */F*

User Information for Server SERVER_MAIN
Connection  User Name        Login Time
----------  -------------    ------------------
     3     * FRED              1/12/89  7:46 pm.

F>
```

3. Turn to Module 85 to continue the learning sequence.

# Module 101

## VOLINFO

### DESCRIPTION

VOLINFO is a public command used to determine the amount of disk space and the number of directory entries used and available on each volume of the current fileserver. This command is vaguely similar to the DOS CHKDSK command, but they are not interchangeable. VOLINFO should always be used on network drives and CHKDSK, on local DOS drives. Under NetWare 2.1 and above, you can select the fileserver on which VOLINFO will report.

### APPLICATIONS

The VOLINFO command is useful to monitor the use of space on network drives. Periodic use of this command helps to determine in advance the need for additional hard drives or the need for housekeeping (removing unneeded files) on existing drives. Use VOLINFO, along with CHKVOL, in place of the less functional CHKDSK found in DOS.

### TYPICAL OPERATION

In this activity, you determine the remaining space on the volumes of the current fileserver. Begin at the DOS prompt of a logged in workstation.

1. Type **VOLINFO** and press **Enter**. The screen displays the following:

| | Total | Free | Total | Free | Total | Free | Total | Free |
|---|---|---|---|---|---|---|---|---|
| Volume name | SYS | | | | | | | |
| KiloBytes | 30808 | 12192 | | | | | | |
| Directories | 2432 | 942 | | | | | | |
| Volume name | | | | | | | | |
| KiloBytes | | | | | | | | |
| Directories | | | | | | | | |
| Volume name | | | | | | | | |
| KiloBytes | | | | | | | | |
| Directories | | | | | | | | |
| Volume name | | | | | | | | |
| KiloBytes | | | | | | | | |
| Directories | | | | | | | | |

Friday January 20, 1989 5:35 pm

This display is periodically refreshed with updated data until interrupted by the user.

2. Press any key to return to the DOS prompt.
3. Turn to Module 21 to continue the learning sequence.

# Module 102

## WHOAMI

### DESCRIPTION

WHOAMI is a public command which displays information about the username under which you are logged in. Your connection number (a number that the fileserver temporarily assigns each user at the time of log in) and the fileservers to which you attached are displayed. You may follow the command with a fileserver name, certain flag, or both. The following flags provide additional information about your current status. The full names or abbreviations can be used. If you wish to use any of these flags, follow the command WHOAMI with a forward slash and then the flag.

| | |
|---|---|
| **A (All)** | This flag displays all information available with WHOAMI. |
| **G (Group)** | This flag lists the GROUPS to which your username currently belongs. |
| **R (Rights)** | This flag displays all of your rights in all directories. This is similar to the information provided by the RIGHTS command (see Module 81). |
| **S (Security)** | This flag lists any security equivalences assigned to your username by SYSCON (see Module 95). |

### APPLICATIONS

Use WHOAMI to determine the username under which you are logged in, as well as your log in time. Also, certain privileges of that username can be displayed. An administrator, for instance, can determine who is logged in to an unattended workstation, or a user that has more than one username can easily determine how they logged in.

### TYPICAL OPERATION

In this activity, you determine how you are logged in and to what groups you belong. Begin at the DOS prompt of a logged in workstation.

1. Type **WHOAMI /G** and press **Enter**. A screen similar to this is displayed:

```
F>WHOAMI /G
You are user FRED attached to server SERVER_MAIN
connection 3.
Login Time:  Thursday January 12, 1989  7:46pm
You are a member of the following Groups:
    EVERYONE (group)

F>
```

2. Turn to Module 100 to continue the learning sequence.

# Appendix A

## TERMS AND DEFINITIONS

### INTRODUCTION

The following list defines terms related to Novell NetWare and networks in general. It is assumed that you have a basic understanding of personal computers and DOS, therefore, basic DOS concepts and terminology are not included. For a comprehensive education in DOS, or for a quick reference guide, see Wordware Publishing's *Illustrated MS/PC-DOS*.

| *Term* | *Definition* |
| --- | --- |
| Administrator | An individual who's job it is to manage the network. This usually includes defining users, groups, print queues, and network security. Administrators are normally given the security equivalence of SUPERVISOR. |
| ARCNET | A popular type of network for use with Novell NetWare. ARCNET uses a token passing scheme and currently transmits data at up to 2.5 megabytes/second. |
| CSMA/CD | Carrier Sense Multiple Access Collision Detection. This is the networking scheme used by Ethernet networks. The NIC detects data collisions on the network and retransmits the data. |
| Console | This refers to the screen and keyboard of a fileserver. On nondedicated fileservers there is a NetWare command called CONSOLE that transfers the system from the workstation mode to the fileserver console mode. |
| Console Command | Any of a number of NetWare commands that are issued from the fileserver console. |
| Console Prompt | The colon that appears at the left edge of the fileserver's screen that indicates that the system is ready for a command to be entered. |
| Dedicated Fileserver | A computer whose only purpose is to be a fileserver. It cannot function as a workstation. |

| Term | Definition |
|---|---|
| ELS | This is a version of Novell NetWare that limits the number of concurrent users to either four (ELS I) or eight (ELS II). ELS stands for Entry Level Solution. |
| Ethernet | A popular type of network for use with Novell NetWare. Ethernet uses a CSMA/CD and currently transmits data at up to 10 megabytes/second. |
| Fileserver | The computer which is the heart of the network. The fileserver contains one or more fixed disks that are shared with the workstations on the network. The fileserver also holds and directs queued print jobs. |
| Fileserver Name | A unique name assigned to each fileserver on a network at the time of installation. |
| Group | A definition of user rights and privileges. Groups are defined, then users are assigned to these groups. One user can be assigned to multiple groups. |
| Log In | The process of using the Login command at a workstation to gain access to the network's resources. This access is limited accordingly to the rights given the username that you use. These rights are established by the network administrator. |
| Log Out | The process of using the Logout command to end a session on a network and, thereby, your ability to access the network's resources. To maintain network security, always log out when leaving your workstation. |
| Multiserver Network | A network with more than one fileserver. Any user on the network may access any fileserver to which they have been assigned a username. |
| NetWare | A network operating system by Novell, Inc. This is the software portion of a Novell network and resides, in part, on both the fileserver and each workstation. |
| NetWare 286 | A version of NetWare that is designed for use on 80286 or 80386 based IBM compatible fileservers. Workstations may be 80386, 80286, 8086, or 8088 based. |
| NetWare 86 | A version of NetWare that is designed for use on 8086 or 8088 based fileservers. While NetWare 86 will run on 80286 or 80386 fileservers, it does not take full advantage of this more recent technology and will not perform as well as NetWare 286. Any type of IBM compatible workstations may be used. |
| NetWare 386 | A version of NetWare designed specifically for 80386 fileservers. See Appendix D. |

| *Term* | *Definition* |
|---|---|
| Network Interface Card | An integrated circuit board that is installed in each fileserver and workstation on a network. It is through this device that the computers communicate along a cabling system. |
| NIC | Abbreviation for network interface card. |
| Node | A workstation, fileserver, communication server, or print server; in other words, any computer that is attached to the network. |
| Nondedicated Fileserver | A computer that has the combined function of both fileserver and workstation. Two commands (CONSOLE and DOS) are used to toggle the system between these modes. This concept is not supported by all versions of NetWare. |
| Public Command | Any of a group of NetWare commands that are issued from network workstations. At the time of installation, NetWare places the commands in a directory called SYS:PUBLIC. |
| Queue | A temporary holding area for print jobs (groups of data that have been sent to network printers). The jobs are accumulated in queues and sent to the appropriate printer as it is ready. |
| Rights | Privileges assigned to users that allow or deny various types of access to network files or directories. Among these are the ability to read, write, delete, and modify files. |
| SFT | This stands for System Fault Tolerant, a version of NetWare that has the ability to continue functioning in spite of certain failures in network hardware. |
| SUPERVISOR | A special username that is automatically created at the time of NetWare installation. SUPERVISOR has all rights to all files and directories, as well as the ability to access all utilities and to change passwords, login scripts, users, groups, etc. Any user may be assigned supervisor equivalency by the SUPERVISOR. |
| System Command | A special group of commands that are issued at network workstations. These commands are located in the SYS:SYSTEM directory. |
| Token Passing | A scheme of network data passing that has each NIC transmitting one at a time. A software "token" is passed from one node to the next, with each NIC only allowed to transmit when it has the token. This concept prevents data collisions. |

| Term | Definition |
|---|---|
| Username | A unique name assigned to each user on the network. Each username is created and defined in terms of privileges and password by the network administrator. |
| Volume | A division of hard drive storage. A volume often consists of the entire drive. Directories are created within the volume, and files are stored within the directories. |
| Wildcard | A DOS concept that applies to many NetWare commands. There are two wildcards, the * and ? characters. When specifying file or directory names, the * can represent any group of missing characters, and the ? any single character. |
| Workstation | The individual computers attached to the network from which users run their applications. They can access shared network resources, such as drives and printers. |
| Workstation Prompt | The standard DOS prompt on the workstation screen which indicates that the computer is ready for its next command. Examples of workstation prompts include "F>" and "G:\Public>." |

# Appendix B
## NOVELL COMMANDS AND SYNTAX

| *Command* | *Syntax* |
|---|---|
| ARCHIVE | ARCHIVE |
| ATOTAL | ATOTAL |
| ATTACH | ATTACH *fileserver/username* |
| BINDFIX | BINDFIX |
| BINDREST | BINDREST |
| BROADCAST | BROADCAST *message* |
| CAPTURE | CAPTURE *option* |
| CASTOFF | CASTOFF *flags* |
| CASTON | CASTON |
| CHANGE QUEUE | CHANGE QUEUE *printer number* JOB *job number* TO PRIORITY *priority number* |
| CHKVOL | CHKVOL *fileserver/volume drive:* |
| CLEAR MESSAGE | CLEAR MESSAGE |
| CLEAR STATION | CLEAR STATION *station number* |
| CONFIG | CONFIG |
| CONSOLE | CONSOLE |
| CPMOFF | CPMOFF |
| CPMON | CPMON |
| DISABLE LOGIN | DISABLE LOGIN |
| DISK | DISK |
| DISMOUNT | DISMOUNT [PACK] *volume number* |
| DOS | DOS |
| DOWN | DOWN |
| ENABLE LOGIN | ENABLE LOGIN |
| ENDCAP | ENDCAP *option* |
| ENDSPOOL | ENDSPOOL |
| EOJOFF | EOJOFF |
| EOJON | EOJON |
| FCONSOLE | FCONSOLE |
| FILER | FILER |
| FLAG | FLAG *directory/filename flags* |
| FORM CHECK | FORM CHECK [PRINTER] *printer number* |
| FORM SET | FORM SET [PRINTER] *printer number* |
| GRANT | GRANT *option* FOR *path* TO *username* |
| HELP | HELP |

| *Command* | *Syntax* |
|---|---|
| HIDEFILE | HIDEFILE *directory/filename* |
| HOLDOFF | HOLDOFF |
| HOLDON | HOLDON |
| KILL PRINTER | KILL PRINTER *printer number* |
| KILL QUEUE | KILL QUEUE *printer number* JOB *job number* |
| LISTDIR | LISTDIR *directory drive:* flags |
| LOGIN | LOGIN *fileserver/username parameter* |
| LOGOUT | LOGOUT *fileserver* |
| MAIL | MAIL |
| MAKEUSER | MAKEUSER |
| MAP | MAP *drive:* = *directory* (see MAP, for more syntaxes) |
| MONITOR | MONITOR *station number* |
| MOUNT | MOUNT [PACK] *volume number* |
| NAME | NAME |
| NCOPY | NCOPY *filename directory/filename* TO *drive:filename directory/drive:* |
| NDIR | NDIR *path option* |
| NPRINT | NPRINT *directory/filename flags* |
| NSNIPES | NSNIPES *skill level* |
| OFF | OFF |
| PAUDIT | PAUDIT |
| PCONSOLE | PCONSOLE |
| PRINTCON | PRINTCON |
| PRINTDEF | PRINTDEF |
| PSTAT | PSTAT *option* |
| PURGE | PURGE |
| QUEUE-212 | Q *entry /flags* |
| *QUEUE-C* | *QUEUE printer number* |
| QUEUE-P | QUEUE |
| REMOVE | REMOVE USER *user* FROM *path* |
| RENDIR | RENDIR *path* TO *directory* |
| REROUTE PRINTER | REROUTE PRINTER *printer number* TO PRINTER *printer number* |
| REVOKE | REVOKE *option* FOR *path* FROM USER *username* |
| REWIND PRINTER | REWIND PRINTER *printer number number of pages* PAGES |
| RIGHTS | RIGHTS *fileserver/drive:directory* |
| SALVAGE | SALVAGE *fileserver/volume:drive:* |
| SECURITY | SECURITY |
| SEND-C | SEND *message* TO STATION *station number* |
| SEND-P | SEND *message* TO *fileserver/username* |
| SESSION | SESSION |
| SET TIME | SET TIME *month/day/year hour:minute:second* |
| SETPASS | SETPASS *fileserver* |
| SHOWFILE | SHOWFILE *directory/filename* |
| SLIST | SLIST |

| *Command* | *Syntax* |
|---|---|
| SMODE | SMODE *path option* |
| SPOOL | SPOOL *flags* |
| START PRINTER | START PRINTER *printer number* |
| STOP PRINTER | STOP PRINTER *printer number* |
| SYSCON | SYSCON |
| SYSTIME | SYSTIME *fileserver* |
| TIME | TIME |
| TLIST | TLIST *path* |
| UDIR | UDIR *directory: filename* |
| USERLIST | USERLIST *fileserver/username* |
| VOLINFO | VOLINFO |
| WHOAMI | WHOAMI *fileserver /flags* |

# Appendix C

## NOVELL NETWARE EXERCISES

1. About This Book
   a. Describe the purpose of NetWare.
   b. How is the Recommended Learning Sequence used?
2. An Overview of a Novell Network
   a. How many versions of Novell exist today?
   b. Can you upgrade from one version to another?
   c. Does each computer on the network need a network interface card?
   d. Under what circumstance can a fileserver become a workstation?
   e. What is a working copy?
   f. Describe the different versions of NetWare.
   g. Would you use a 16-bit computer as a fileserver?
   h. Should you have a hard drive in the fileserver?
   i. What is a UPS?
3. Hardware Installation
   a. Can NICs have the same address setting?
4. COMPSURF
   a. What is does the COMPSURF utility do?
   b. How long can COMPSURF take to finish?
   c. With NetWare 286 versions 2.1 and above, how do you invoke COMPSURF?
5. NET$OS
   a. What is NET$OS?
   b. How is NET$OS generated with NetWare 286?
   c. How is NET$OS generated with ELS NetWare 286?
6. INSTALL
   a. Is INSTALL used before or after COMPSURF?
   b. Can INSTALL ever be used again?
7. START
   a. Which version of NetWare uses START?
   b. When would you use START?

8. Workstation Shells (ANET)
   a. During GENSH, should you use the original diskettes?
   b. Will NetWare run under all versions of DOS?
   c. Which shell would you use under ELS NetWare 286?
9. Troubleshooting
   a. What do you look for if the drive will not format?
   b. Will a defective chip show up during fileserver boot?
   c. What is caching?
10. Booting the System
    a. What is involved in booting the system?
    b. What is involved in booting the fileserver?
    c. What is a diskless workstation?
    d. Explain bringing a workstation and fileserver down.
11. ARCHIVE
    a. What is meant by ARCHIVing?
    b. Explain the difference between NARCHIVE and LARCHIVE.
    c. What DOS command is replaced by ARCHIVE?
12. ATOTAL
    a. Is ATOTAL valid in all versions of NetWare?
    b. Can you obtain a hard copy?
13. ATTACH
    a. Is ATTACH used before or after LOGIN?
    b. Would you use this command with only one fileserver?
14. BINDFIX
    a. What is a bindery?
    b. What does BINDFIX do first?
    c. Can you run this utility at any time without affecting users?
15. BINDREST
    a. What is BINDREST used for?
    b. List the two files that must be present for BINDREST to work.
16. BROADCAST
    a. Is BROADCAST done from a workstation?
    b. How is the screen cleared from a workstation?
17. CAPTURE
    a. What is the command replaced by CAPTURE?
    b. Which flag makes any number of copies?
    c. Which flag restores automatic form feeds?
    d. What is NB?
    e. Which flag would you use to cause immediate printing while in an application?

18. CASTOFF
    a. What is CASTOFF?
    b. Which flag would cause messages from only workstations to be disabled?
19. CASTON
    a. What command does CASTON negate?
    b. Are there any flags available?
20. CHANGE QUEUE
    a. Is CHANGE QUEUE available to a workstation?
    b. Explain what each of the three variables are.
21. CHKVOL
    a. Which DOS command does CHKVOL replace?
    b. Explain what can be found using CHKVOL.
22. CLEAR MESSAGE
    a. Can Ctrl-Enter be used to clear messages from a console?
23. CLEAR STATION
    a. Why would you most commonly use CLEAR STATION?
    b. What is the syntax of the command?
24. CONFIG
    a. Which information is provided by CONFIG?
    b. Will it list the type?
25. CONSOLE
    a. What is a nondedicated fileserver?
    b. Can workstation commands be used from a console?
26. CPMOFF
    a. Explain the purpose of CPMOFF.
    b. Will it affect all workstations?
27. CPMON
    a. What command does CPMON negate?
28. DISABLE LOGIN
    a. Can DISABLE LOGIN be used from a workstation?
    b. If you are logged in, will this command affect you?
29. DISK
    a. What information is displayed after the drive number?
    b. Which command will discontinue the display?

30. DISMOUNT
    a. What is DISMOUNT informing NetWare?
    b. Which command should be used for diskettes?

31. DOS
    a. Why would you use the command DOS?
    b. Would this command be used on a dedicated fileserver?

32. DOWN
    a. Should workstations be logged in when using DOWN?
    b. Explain what DOWN is actually doing.
    c. Should a network ever be shut off without issuing DOWN?

33. ENABLE LOGIN
    a. What command does ENABLE LOGIN negate?
    b. Is this command issued from a workstation?

34. ENDCAP
    a. Is this command valid in all versions of NetWare?
    b. What would happen if this command were issued: ENDCAP/CL = 2?

35. ENDSPOOL
    a. What does ENDSPOOL accomplish?
    b. What does the C flag do?
    c. Is ENDSPOOL valid in all versions of NetWare?

36. EOJOFF
    a. What happens when an "end of job" is issued?
    b. What does EOJOFF prevent?

37. EOJON
    a. What is the default?
    b. What does EOJON assure you of?

38. FCONSOLE
    a. Do you need supervisor privileges to BROADCAST?
    b. Which menu selection provides a list of those connected?
    c. Can you DOWN the fileserver through FCONSOLE?
    d. What does the menu selection Statistics tell you?

39. FILER
    a. What are trustees?
    b. What information cannot be changed through the File Information selection?

40. FLAG
   a. What will happen if a path or filename is not specified?
   b. Which flag would be used to prevent users from modifying specified files?
   c. When is the S flag used?
41. FORM CHECK
   a. Give an example of the syntax of FORM CHECK.
   b. Which command is used once the form is aligned?
42. FORM SET
   a. Give an example of the syntax of FORM SET.
43. GRANT
   a. Is GRANT available in all versions of NetWare?
   b. In which menu utility is GRANT also found?
   c. Give an example of the syntax of GRANT.
44. HELP
   a. Can you access HELP from any directory?
   b. How do you exit HELP?
45. HIDEFILE
   a. Does HIDEFILE protect a file from deletion?
   b. Can wildcards be used?
46. HOLDOFF
   a. What command is negated by HOLDOFF?
47. HOLDON
   a. Can users modify a file locked by HOLDON?
48. KILL PRINTER
   a. Can KILL PRINTER be executed from a workstation?
   b. What is the default printer?
49. KILL QUEUE
   a. Can KILL QUEUE be executed from a workstation?
   b. Will resetting the printer delete a print job?
50. LISTDIR
   a. Which DOS command is similar to LISTDIR?
   b. Which flag would be used to have the creation date and time displayed?
51. LOGIN
   a. Will there always be a password for every user?
   b. Under what circumstance(s) would you not specify a server?

52. LOGIN SCRIPTS
    a. Can LOGIN SCRIPTS be assigned with MAKEUSER?
    b. Who can change the SYSTEM LOGIN SCRIPT?
53. LOGOUT
    a. When is it not necessary to specify a server?
    b. Should you LOGOUT even if only leaving your workstation for a few minutes?
54. MAIL
    a. What is a memo?
    b. Which command will tell you if any mail has been sent to you?
    c. How do you exit the MAIL utility?
55. MAKEUSER
    a. Which menu utility could also be used in place of MAKEUSER?
    b. Which extension must be given to the text file?
56. MAP
    a. Which DOS command is similar to MAP?
    b. Can drive names be any letter?
57. MENU
    a. What is the syntax for MENU?
    b. What extension must the text file have?
58. MONITOR
    a. Can MONITOR be displayed from a workstation?
    b. Which information will be displayed?
59. MOUNT
    a. What does MOUNT inform NetWare?
    b. What command should be used with fileservers that use disk packs?
60. NAME
    a. Which DOS command is similar to NAME?
61. NCOPY
    a. Give an example of the syntax of NCOPY.
62. NDIR
    a. Which command should be used for versions 2.0 and below?
    b. Which flag will list files last accessed by a user?
    c. List all of the attribute flags.
63. NPRINT
    a. Which DOS command is similar to NPRINT?
    b. Why is this faster than the DOS command?

64. NSNIPES
    a. Play a game of NSNIPES.
65. OFF
    a. Which command does this negate?
    b. Can this command be issued from a workstation?
66. PAUDIT
    a. Under what circumstances is PAUDIT valid?
    b. How do you receive a hard copy of this report?
    c. Should this file always be there?
67. PCONSOLE
    a. Which command did PCONSOLE replace?
    b. List the things you can do to a queue by PCONSOLE.
    c. What selection lists users currently allowed to use the queue?
68. PRINTCON
    a. Is PRINTCON valid with all versions of NetWare?
    b. Which menu selection allows you to copy a user's set of configuration to another user?
69. PRINTDEF
    a. What is usually the first character of a control code?
    b. What information is needed to create a form?
70. PRINTER
    a. What is a queue?
    b. How would you list the jobs in queue SALES?
71. PSTAT
    a. If the P= flag is omitted, what will PSTAT report?
    b. Can this be executed from a workstation?
72. PURGE
    a. Besides PURGE, what else will cause the deletion of files marked for deletion?
73. QUEUE (CONSOLE 2.1)
    a. Which QUEUE command deletes all waiting print jobs in a specified queue?
74. QUEUE (CONSOLE)
    a. What follows the command QUEUE?
75. QUEUE (PUBLIC)
    a. Is this command the same as the console command of the same name?

76. REMOVE
    a. Under NetWare 2.1 and above, what does this command remove?
    b. What menu-driven utility provides users the same ability as REMOVE?

77. RENDIR
    a. What does this command do to directories?
    b. What two rights must a user have in order to use RENDIR?

78. REROUTE PRINTER
    a. From where must this command be issued?
    b. What is the syntax for this command?

79. REVOKE
    a. What does this command remove?
    b. Is REVOKE used on users or groups?

80. REWIND PRINTER
    a. How far back is the queue rewound if the number of pages is not specified?
    b. What is the maximum number of pages you can rewind?

81. RIGHTS
    a. What menu-driven utility provides you with the same information as RIGHTS?
    b. Which right allows you to list files in a directory?
    c. Which right allows you to prepare a file for access?

82. SALVAGE
    a. Can you SALVAGE files that have been PURGEd?
    b. If a path or filename is not specified, what is SALVAGEd?

83. SECURITY
    a. What does SECURITY do?
    b. How do you obtain a hard copy of this report?

84. SEND (CONSOLE)
    a. Which command is SEND (console) similar to?
    b. Omission of workstation numbers causes the message to be sent to whom?

85. SEND (PUBLIC)
    a. Where is the message displayed?
    b. How is a message cleared?

86. SESSION
    a. Which menu selection allows you to determine your default drive?
    b. List the NetWare command being accomplished through each menu selection.

87. SET TIME
    a. Will this command change a workstation's time?
    b. What would be the correct entry for 3:00 p.m.?
88. SETPASS
    a. What menu-driven utility will also let you assign a password?
    b. If you already have a password, will SETPASS allow you to change it?
89. SHOWFILE
    a. What command does SHOWFILE reverse?
    b. Can you use wildcards in naming a file to show?
90. SLIST
    a. What will SLIST list?
    b. Would you use this command on a single-server network?
91. SMODE
    a. Explain where NetWare will search if mode 1 is used.
92. SPOOL
    a. Does NetWare direct printer output straight to the appropriate queue?
    b. If a banner is not desired, what flag would be used?
    c. What will happen if the flag NFF is used?
93. START PRINTER
    a. Can this command be executed from a workstation?
    b. Which commands does START PRINTER reverse?
94. STOP PRINTER
    a. When this command is issued, will the printer stop immediately?
    b. When the printer is restarted, will the print job start over at the beginning?
95. SYSCON
    a. What options are available under Supervisor Options?
    b. What does "accounting" track?
96. SYSTIME
    a. Does this command "only" display the current time and date?
97. TIME
    a. Can this command be done from a workstation?
98. TLIST
    a. What is a trustee?
    b. If neither USER or GROUP is used, what is listed?

99. UDIR
    a. Can wildcards be used?
    b. Which command replaced UDIR?

100. USERLIST
    a. When is this command commonly used?
    b. What is listed on the screen beside the list of users?

101. VOLINFO
    a. What DOS command is similar to VOLINFO?
    b. Can VOLINFO be used on local drives?

102. WHOAMI
    a. What flag will display any security equivalences assigned to your username?

# Appendix D
## NETWARE 386

### DESCRIPTION

In late 1989 Novell released its most powerful network operating system to date. Called NetWare 386, the system is designed to run on fileservers based on the Intel 80386 microprocessor. It will also run on "upwardly compatible" systems such as the 80486. Workstations, as with other NetWare operating systems, can be almost any IBM compatible PC.

The 80386 has two basic modes of operation. The "real" mode is the standard single-task type of operation found in the original Intel 8088. Typical DOS-based software uses this mode. The "protected" mode allows advanced processor-level multitasking. That is, multiple operations can take place concurrently and independent of each other. NetWare 386 uses the protected mode to provide power, ease of configuration and modification, and system fault tolerance. In addition, NetWare 386 is written to take full advantage of the 80386 instruction set. This is a more extensive and powerful set of commands than that of previous microprocessors. Thus, NetWare 386 is much faster than Advanced NetWare.

### STRUCTURE

NetWare 386 can only be run in a dedicated mode (see page 5). The server, however, must first load DOS before running the NetWare operating system. This may be done either from a floppy diskette, or a DOS partition on the first hard drive. The operating system is a DOS executable file called SERVER.EXE. Server is used not only for fileserver operation, but also to install and modify the system.

Once SERVER is loaded, various programs are loaded—each running as an independent task. These programs are called NLMs, or NetWare Loadable Modules, and all have the extension NLM. A program called INSTALL.NLM is used to compsurf, format, partition, mirror and duplex drives, install system files, and perform various configuration tasks.

There are NLMs that interface with various types of hard drive controllers. Novell provides these for standard AT controllers (including MFM, RLL, and ESDI formats), IBM Micro Channel controllers, SCSI (Small Computer Standard Interface) controllers, and others. Other NLMs interface with whatever network interface cards are in use. Those that Novell provides include ARCnet, Ethernet, and Token Ring. Because of NetWare 386's open architecture, other vendors can provide proprietary NLMs for drives and NICs.

For each NIC and drive controller in the server, an NLM must be loaded. Information such as the address and interrupt settings for these cards is specified each time the appropriate NLM is loaded. If, for example, you have three ARCnet NICs in the server, the ARCnet.NLM module is loaded three times—each time with different settings. The order in which NLMs are loaded can be important. SERVER.EXE allows you to create configuration scripts that run each time the server is booted. This way all of the needed NLMs are loaded with the proper settings and in the proper order.

NLMs can be loaded and unloaded as needed without downing the server. This new structure has many advantages. There is no longer a need to generate and link the operating system. Instead you simply create and modify the configuration scripts. You can compsurf, format, and partition a drive while the server and its other drives are running. With external drives, this means defective units can actually be replaced without ever interrupting work on the other drives!

In NetWare 386 the CONSOLE command MONITOR (see Module 58) is replaced with MONITOR.NLM. This module provides more extensive information than previous versions of NetWare. There is also a screen-save feature built in. If no keys are pressed for several minutes, the screen clears and a sort of graphic "comet" begins bouncing across the screen so users do not think the fileserver is down. Once any key is pressed, the monitor display returns.

The diskettes that come with NetWare 386 are either 1.2 megabyte 5 ¼" or 1.44 megabyte 3 ½". You cannot use a server that does not have a high capacity floppy drive. This has allowed Novell to lower the number of diskettes from dozens to about 10. The first diskette, labeled SYSTEM, contains SERVER.EXE and the NLMs. Additional diskettes contain all of the system and public programs and utilities. As always, it is important to make working copies of the diskettes and store the originals in a safe place.

## INSTALLATION

First time installations of NetWare 386 are far simpler and quicker than with previous versions of NetWare. Aside from drive preparation, the installation and configuration of a fileserver can often be done in as little as an hour. Because the structure of NetWare 386 is so different from previous versions, the most difficult task can be attaining a full understanding of the system. Fortunately, the documentation has also been upgraded, and a quick review of the installation manual may be all that is required.

Existing Novell networks may be upgraded to NetWare 386. There is a menu-driven utility supplied with NetWare 386 called UPGRADE that makes this a fairly easy task. You can attach a new fileserver to the existing network and use UPGRADE to transfer all existing files across the network from the old fileserver. Or you can specify a tape backup attached to a workstation to which UPGRADE will transfer all files. Either way, the files are converted into NetWare 386 format. This is particularly important for the bindery files which have considerably different structures. In the case of the tape backup upgrade, the new NetWare is installed on the old drives, then the files are restored. If the old drives were running Advanced Netware, there is no need to re-compsurf them.

## PRINTERS

With NetWare 386 Novell introduced a whole new level of shared printer management. Shared printers no longer have to be connected directly to a fileserver. Any printer attached to any workstation can be shared. This is accomplished through a program called PSERVER. This is provided as both an NLM and a DOS executable file. For each copy of PSERVER running on the network, you can attach 16 printers. The DOS executable PSERVER must be run from a dedicated workstation. For this reason, networks with 16 or less printers normally will only use the NLM. The advantages of managing printers in this manner are so great that Novell has included similar abilities in Advanced NetWare version 2.15 revision D and above. In this case, PSERVER is a VAP (Value Added Process) that runs at the server.

## SALVAGING/PURGING FILES

With previous versions of NetWare deleted files can be salvaged (see Module 82) as long as no other file operations are executed first, and the user remains logged in. NetWare 386 retains all deleted files as long as there is sufficient storage capacity in the volume. Other files can be deleted, created, opened and closed, the user can login and logout, and the fileserver can even be downed. This means a deleted file could actually be retrieved months later!

Once the total of existing files and deleted files reaches the capacity of the volume, the oldest delete files are physically erased as needed.

## SECURITY IMPROVEMENTS

NetWare 386 provides several significant enhancements to network security. Trustee rights can now be assigned not only to directories, but to individual files. This greatly enhances the administrator's ability to determine who can access what information.

A user can now be given supervisor rights at a given directory level. In other words, the manager of a sales department might be made a supervisor of the directory MAIN/SYS:SALES. Within this directory, and any subdirectories that it contains, this user would have full supervisory rights.

Furthermore, a user (or user group) can be made a group manager. This provides supervisor control over a given group of users. Both of these enhancements are controlled through the SYSCON menu-driven utility.

## WORKGROUP MANAGERS

NetWare 386 allows the designation of a given user or user group as manager of other users and/or groups. The workgroup manager is a sub-supervisor. Whatever trustee rights the manager has can be assigned to anyone in their workgroup. They can also create users and groups to add to their workgroup. They cannot create other workgroup managers. Workgroup management is set up through SYSCON.

As an example of the use of workgroup managers, consider an accounting department within a corporation. The controller can be made a workgroup manager with trustee rights to all applications and data used by the accounting department. The controller can then create whatever users and groups needed within the department, assigning them whatever trustee rights are appropriate for their job. This relieves the system administrator of dealing with individual users.

## MAPPING ENHANCEMENTS

An important new option has been added to the MAP function. This can be implemented either through the public command MAP (Module 56) or through LOGIN SCRIPTS (Module 52). You can now specify that a given directory will appear as the root directory of the named drive letter. For example, the above named directory, MAIN/SYS:SALES, can be mapped to S:\. When the current default drive is S:, the DOS command CD\ cannot be used to return you to the root directory of SYS:. This is particularly useful when dealing with software applications that must be run from predetermined drive and directory specifications. Its effect is similar to the DOS command SUBST, which cannot be used with NetWare. The syntax is MAP ROOT d: = f/p where d is the new root directory name, f is the name of the actual fileserver, and p is the full path of the old directory.

## NEW COMMANDS

**ALLOW** This public command assigns and removes rights to the Inherited Rights Mask for specified directories and files. This, along with trustee assignments, determines if and in what manner a user can access a file. In NetWare 386 there are eight assignable rights. The following is a list of these rights, their Advanced NetWare equivalents, and their function.

**NetWare 386 File Rights**

| *NetWare 386 Right* | *Advanced NetWare Equivalent* | *NetWare 386 Function* |
|---|---|---|
| Supervisory | —none— | Complete control of this directory and all files and subdirectories below it. |
| Read | Read | Open and read files. Advanced NetWare had a separate Open right. |
| Write | Write | Open and write to files. |
| Create | Create | Create, open, and write to files. |
| Erase | Delete | Delete a file, directory, or entire directory structure. |
| Modify | Modify | Change file and directory attributes or names. |
| File Scan | Search | List file in directory (like DOS DIR). |
| Access Control | —none— | Allows a user to give whatever rights they have for the specified file or directory to other users. |

The command syntax is

ALLOW fileserver/directory/filename rights

Specify fileserver and directory only if different from the current default. If assigning rights to a specific file, include the filename. You can list one or more rights, using the first letter of each right.

If a previously ALLOWED right is not included in the list, it will be removed. To grant all rights, you can use All; to remove all rights use Nothing.

**DSPACE** This is a menu-driven utility that allows you to limit the disk space available to given users. You can specify the total kilobytes for a given volume or directory.

**FLAGDIR** Similar to the FLAG command, but is used to set attributes for directories. The FLAG command is discussed in Module 40. Changes to FLAG under NetWare 386 are discussed later in this appendix. NetWare 386 directories can have the following six attributes.

**NetWare 386 Directory Attributes**

| | |
|---|---|
| DELETE | Removes the ability for any user to delete this directory. |
| HIDDEN | Hides the directory so that it is not included when using the DOS command DIR (or the NetWare command NDIR). This also prevents it from being copied or deleted. |
| NORMAL | Cancels all other attributes. |
| PURGE | Causes files in this directory to be purged immediately when they are deleted. In other words, they are physically erased from the directory and cannot be salvaged. |
| RENAME | Removes the ability for any user to rename this directory. |
| SYSTEM | Indicates that files within this directory are vital to system operation. The directory cannot be deleted or copied. It is hidden from the DOS command DIR, but can be listed with NDIR. |

The command syntax is

```
FLAGDIR fileserver/directory attributes
```

To view the current attributes of a file, omit the attributes list in the above syntax.

**NBACKUP** This menu-driven utility allows you to backup and restore fileserver data to any DOS device. This can be a local hard drive, floppy drive, or any device that has a DOS driver available for it. This includes many tape backup systems as well as most optical disk drives. This sophisticated system replaces the older ARCHIVE commands (Module 11).

**PSC** This public command allows similar control of network printers that was previously only available at the fileserver console (Module 70). To control a given printer, you must be established as a Print Server Operator. The command syntax is

PSC PS = printserver P = printer FLAGS

**PS** is the name of any valid printserver. This can be a fileserver running PSERVER.NLM or a dedicated workstation running PSERVER.EXE. P is the number assigned to the actual printer. The following are valid flags:

**NetWare 386 Printer Control**

| | |
|---|---|
| ABORT | Halt the current print job. |
| CANCEL DOWN | Down the print server. |
| FORM FEED | Move paper one page. |
| MARK | Mark the paper's position. |
| MOUNT FORM = | Specify a new form. |
| PAUSE | Pause the printer. |
| RIVATE | Reserve the printer for your use only. |
| REWIND x | Back up x number of pages in the current print job. |
| SHARED | Make printer available to others on the network. |
| START | Restart a STOPped printer. |
| STATUS | Report current printer status. |
| STOP | Stop output to a printer, but maintain all print jobs. |

**PSERVER** This public command dedicates a workstation as a printserver. If you do not want to use PSERVER.NLM at the fileserver, or if you need more than 16 shared printers, it will be necessary to use this command. Once it is run, the workstation cannot be used for other applications unless it is reset. For each workstation running PSERVER an additional 16 shared printers may be defined on the network. These printers may be attached to any workstation on the network. The command syntax is

PSERVER *printservername*

**RPRINTER** This menu-driven utility makes local printers (those physically attached to your workstation) available to the network. You specify which local printer you want to share and a valid printserver name. The printserver will control the printer and make it available to other users. Remember, a printserver can only control up to 16 printers.

**USERDEF** This menu-driven utility allows easy creation and definition of new users. Many of the use functions provided with SYSCON are available with USERDEF. But with USERDEF you can create custom "templates" that predefines the user. For example, the template can specify user login scripts, home directories, and account restrictions. When creating a new user, simply specify the appropriate template.

## CHANGED COMMANDS

**FILER** The menu structure of this utility has been arranged differently. In older versions, the main menu of FILER had separate options for "File Information" and "Subdirectory Information" (see Module 39). These have been combined. The menu option is now called "Directory Contents."

More importantly, FILER now allows you to perform a given operation on multiple files or directories at the same time. When viewing the contents of a directory, you can use the F5 key to mark multiple entries. Each entry that is marked will blink. When all desired entries are marked, press Enter. A menu will appear, giving you the choice of copying or modifying all marked items in a number of different ways.

Finally the new FILER uses NetWare 386's revised set of file and directory rights and directory attributes (see ALLOW and FLAGDIR, respectively, earlier in this appendix).

**GRANT** This public command works the same as described in Module 43, but now with the NetWare 386 set of rights.

**MAP** This public command has the added option of "MAP ROOT" as discussed earlier in this appendix.

**REVOKE** This public command works the same as described in Module 43, but now with the NetWare 386 set of rights.

**RIGHTS** This public command works the same as described in Module 81, but now with the NetWare 386 set of rights.

**SALVAGE** This public command can often restore deleted files even after the user has logged out or the server has been downed. A full explanation can be found earlier in this appendix.

**SYSCON** This menu-driven utility offers the same functions as before (Module 95), but with the added ability of defining workgroup management. When you select a user or group from the list, two new options are available. One designates the user or group as a workgroup manager over whichever users or groups you select. The other adds the user or group to whichever managed groups you select.

# Index


**ABEND**, 30
ACCESS, 130, 132
ACCESS DENIED, 102
ACCOUNT EXPIRATION, 115
Accounting, 39, 115, 140, 200, 230
Add A Queue To A Printer, 151, 168, 198
Administrator, 215
Advanced NetWare, 4, 19, 27
Alignment Pattern, 87
All (flag), 50, 213
ALLOW, 236-237
AM/PM, 107
ANET.COM, 27, 31-32, 74
ARCHIVE, 35, 235
ARCNET, 9, 11, 215, 233
ATOTAL, 39, 223
ATTACH, 40, 104, 183-184, 223
Attributes, 85
AUTO ENDCAP, 45, 146
AUTOEXEC.BAT, 104

**BACKUP**, 35
Bad Disks Blocks, 63
Banner, 45, 133, 193
BANNER FILE, 145
BANNER NAME, 145
Baud Rate, 23
Bindery, 42-43
BINDFIX, 41-43, 223
BINDREST, 41-43, 223
Boot ROM, 8, 32
BREAK ON/OFF, 104
Bridge, 8
BRIEF, 131
BROADCAST, 44, 76, 180, 223, 225
Buffer, 9

**Cable**, 11
CABLING, 8
Cache, 23
CAPTURE, 45, 48-49, 70, 141, 144-146, 148, 160, 193, 223
CASTOFF, 44, 50-52, 224
CASTON, 52, 224
Catching, 7, 30, 67, 223
Change A Queue's Priority, 151
Change Current Fileserver, 76, 183, 200
Change Current Printer, 162
Change Forms, 153
CHANGE QUEUE, 53, 224
CHECK, 110
CHKDSK, 211
CHKVOL, 55, 224
CLEAR, 117
CLEAR MESSAGE, 56, 224
CLEAR STATION, 57, 68, 224
CLOSE, 89, 110, 170, 205
Cold Boot Loader, 22, 31
COMMAND.COM, 104
COMPAQ DeskPro, 6, 286
COMPSURF, 13-16, 19, 22, 24, 29, 224
COMSPEC, 104
CONFIG, 58, 224
Confirm Deletions, 80
Confirm File Copies, 80
Confirm File Overwrites, 80
Connection Information, 76
CONNECTIONS, 115
CONSOLE, 31, 59, 66, 215, 224, 233
Console Command, 215
Console Prompt, 32, 215
Copies, 45, 129, 133, 193
COPY, 129
Copy-Protection, 4
CPMOFF, 60-61, 224
CPMON, 61, 224
CREATE, 46, 117, 130, 132, 152, 174, 193-194
Create A Queue, 152

CSMA/CD, 9, 215
Current Directory Information, 79
Current Print Jobs Entries, 141
Current Queue Status, 141
Currently Attached Server, 141

**Date**, 186, 203-204, 230
DAY, 107
DAY_OF_MONTH, 107
DAY_OF_WEEK, 107
Dedicated Fileservers, 5, 17, 31, 215, 232
DEL, 157, 176
DELETE, 89, 98, 117, 133, 170, 174, 205
Delete A Job In A Queue, 152
Delete A Queue, 152
Destroy A Queue, 152
DEVICE, 146
Device Models, 149
DIR, 207
Directories Exclude Pattern, 80
DIRECTORIESONLY, 130
DIRECTORY, 110
Directory Name, 166
Disable, 194
DISABLE LOGIN, 62, 69, 224
DISK, 139, 224
Disk Blocks, 227
DISKCOPY, 4
Diskless Workstations, 32
DISMOUNT, 65, 127, 225
DISMOUNT PACK, 65
Display Print Queue, 162
Display Printer Information, 162
DISPLAY/FDISPLAY, 104
DOCUMENT, 110
DOS, 31, 66, 225
DOS BREAK ON/OFF, 105
DOS SET, 105
DOS VERIFY ON/OFF, 105
DOWN, 32, 67-68, 225
Down Fileserver, 76
DRIVE, 105
Drive Mappings, 183
Drive Type, 29
DSPACE, 237

**EDIT**, 110
Edit Print Devices, 149
ELS NetWare, 5-7, 13, 17-19, 24, 27, 30, 32, 63, 216, 222
ELSGEN, 13, 17, 151
Enable (flag), 194
ENABLE LOGIN, 62, 69, 225
ENABLE TIMEOUT, 146
End Of Job, 225
ENDCAP (flag), 45, 48, 70, 72, 146, 225
ENDSPOOL, 70, 72, 193, 195, 225
ENVIROMENTAL VARIABLES, 105
EOJOFF, 74-75, 225
EOJON, 74-75, 225
ERASE, 157, 176
Ethernet, 9, 11, 216, 233
ExecutableOnly, 131
EXIT, 105
Export Print Device, 149
Extended Memory, 7

**FCONSOLE**, 76-77, 225
FILE, 110
File Allocation Tables, 4
FILE CONTENTS, 145
File Exclude Pattern, 80
File Include Pattern, 80
File Information, 79
File Search Attributes, 80
File Server Information, 201
FILE SERVER, 146
File/Lock Activity, 76
FILENAME, 131-132
FILER, 79, 81-83, 225, 239
Fileserver, 3, 6-7, 13, 19, 23, 29, 30-32, 59, 67
Fileserver Mode, 59, 66
Fileserver Name, 23
FILESERVER RAM, 7
Fileserver's Clock, 186
Fileserver's Date, 186
FILESONLY, 131
FIRE PHASERS, 105
FLAG, 45, 85-86, 226
FLAGDIR, 237
Floppy Drive, 8
FORM CHECK, 87-88, 226
FORM FEED, 46, 135, 194
FORM NAME, 145
FORM SET, 46, 87-88, 226
Forms, 46, 133, 194
FULL_NAME, 106

**Game**, 137
GENOS, 17
GENSH, 27
GRANT, 89, 90, 165, 170, 174, 226, 239
GREETING_TIME, 107
Group, 115, 213, 216
Group Information, 201
GUEST, 48, 134, 146, 195

**Hard Drive Controller**, 29-30
HARD DRIVES, 6, 8
HELP, 91-92, 110, 226
HIDDEN, 80, 131
HIDEFILE, 94, 189, 226
HOLDOFF, 96-97, 226
HOLDON, 96-97, 226
HOME DIRECTORY, 116
Hot Fix, 5, 63
HOUR, 107
HOUR24, 107

**IBM PC XT**, 6
IBM PS/2, 6
Import Print Device, 149
INCLUDE, 105
Indexed, 131
INSTALL, 19, 23, 134, 195, 222
INSTALL.NLM, 232
Interface Cards, 58
Interleave, 14
IPX.COM, 27, 31-32, 102

**Job**, 46, 135

**Keep**, 46
Key Device, 4
KILL PRINTER, 98, 198, 226
KILL QUEUE, 99, 226

**LAN Driver Information**, 77
LARCHIVE, 35-36, 223
LETTER, 110
LIST, 110
List A Queue's Jobs, 152
List All Queues, 152
List Queues On A Printer, 152
LISTDIR, 100-101, 226
Local, 47, 194
Local Hard Drive, 8
LOCAL PRINTER, 146
Log In, 216
Log Out, 216
LOGIN, 4, 40, 70, 72, 102-103, 109, 223, 226
LOGIN_NAME, 106
LOGIN SCRIPT, 40, 102, 104, 107-108, 116, 166, 191, 227
LOGOUT, 70, 72, 102, 227
LRESTORE, 35, 37

**MACHINE**, 106
MACHINE NAME, 105
MAIL, 110-114, 227
MAIN.MNU, 122, 124
MAKEUSER, 108, 115, 117-118, 121, 227
MAP, 105, 119-121, 183, 191-192, 227, 235-236, 239
MAP ROOT, 235-236
Mark Top of Form, 153
MAX DISK SPACE, 116
MEMO, 110, 227
MENU, 122-124, 227
Message, 180
MINUTE, 107
Mirrored Disks, 5
MNU, 122
MODE, 147
Modified, 131
MODIFY, 89, 170, 174, 205
MONITOR, 57, 125-127, 139
MONITOR.NLM, 233
MONTH, 107
MONTH_NAME, 107
MOUNT, 127, 227
MOUNT PACK, 127
Multiserver Networks, 40, 109, 216

**NAME**, 47, 128, 135, 223, 227
NARCHIVE, 223
NBACKUP, 238
NCOPY, 129, 133, 227
NDAY_OF_WEEK, 107
NDIR, 130, 132, 207, 227
NET$ACCT.DAT, 140
NET$BIND.OLD, 41, 43
NET$BVAL.OLD, 41, 43
NET$OS, 17-18, 27, 31, 222

NETBIOS, 105
NETGEN, 13, 17, 19, 151
NetWare, 4-6, 68, 86, 216, 286
NetWare Interface Card (NIC), 3, 6-8, 17, 23, 27, 30, 32, 217
NetWare 386, 232-240
Network Loadable Module, 232
NETx.COM, 31-32, 74, 102
NEW MAIL, 106
NIC, 233
NLM, 232
No Banner, 47, 134, 194
No Form Feed, 47, 134, 195
NO HOT, 63
No Tabs, 47, 134, 195
NoAutoendcap, 47
Node, 217
Non-Shareable, 85
Nondedicated Fileservers, 7, 17, 59, 66, 217, 224
Normal, 85
NPRINT, 45, 46, 70, 72, 133, 135, 141, 144-145, 148, 160, 162, 193, 227
NUMBER OF COPIES, 145

**OFF**, 139, 228
OPEN, 89, 111, 170, 174, 205
OS, 107
OS_VERSION, 107
OWNER, 131-132

**P_STATION**, 106
Parallel, 23
PARENTAL, 89, 107, 174, 205
Parity, 23
Partition Table, 22
Password, 40, 102-103, 117, 178, 187-188, 201, 230
Password Length, 116
PATH, 119-120, 192
PAUDIT, 140, 228
PAUSE, 105
PCONSOLE, 141-143, 151, 162
PRINT, 133
PRINT BANNER, 145
Print Devices, 148-149
Print Jobs, 54, 98-99, 144, 168, 172-173, 226, 230
Print Queue ID, 141
Print Queues, 141, 146, 151, 159, 172
PRINTCON, 46, 144, 147, 228
PRINTDEF, 134, 145, 148, 150, 153, 160, 228
Printer, 23, 47, 87-88, 98-99, 134-136, 151, 153, 155-156, 160, 168, 191, 193, 195, 199, 228, 230
PrintQ_O, 47, 135, 146
Protected Mode, 232
PSC, 238
PSERVER, 234, 238-239
PSTAT, 155, 228
PUBLIC, 4, 217
PURGE, 157, 176, 228-229, 234-235
Purge All Salvageable Files, 77
PURGE USER DIRECTORY, 116
PUT, 111

**QUEUE**, 47, 54, 98, 135, 141, 151, 153, 159, 160-164, 199, 217, 228, 230
QUEUE (CONSOLE), 160, 228
QUEUE DELETE, 99, 199
QUEUE DESTROY, 98
Queue Operators, 142
QUEUE (PUBLIC), 162, 228
Queue Servers, 142
Queue Users, 142
QUIT, 111

**RAM**, 7, 12, 23, 30, 67
RAM (Fileserver), 7
RAM (Workstation), 8
READ, 89, 111, 170, 174, 205
Read/Only, 85, 131, 191
Read/Write, 85, 131
REMARK, 106
Removable Media, 65
REMOVE, 89, 111, 165, 170, 229
Rename, 166
RENDIR, 166-167, 229
REROUTE PRINTER, 168-169, 198, 229
RESTORE, 35
RESTRICTED TIME, 116
REVERSE, 131
REVOKE, 170-171, 229, 239
REWIND, 199
REWIND PRINTER, 153, 172-173, 229
Rights, 89-90, 166, 170, 174-175, 178, 201, 205, 213, 217, 229
ROM BIOS, 30
RPRINTER, 239

**SALVAGE**, 157-158, 176-177, 229, 234-235, 240
SEARCH, 89, 119, 170, 174, 205
Search Mappings, 183
SECOND, 107
SECURITY, 178-179, 213, 229
Select Current Directory, 80
Select Default Drive, 183
SEND, 44, 51-52, 102, 111, 180-183, 229
SEND (CONSOLE), 180, 229
SEND (PUBLIC), 181, 229
Serial, 23
Server, 48, 134, 155, 195
SERVER.EXE, 232
SESSION, 181, 183-185, 229
Set Filer Options, 80
SET TIME, 186, 230
SETPASS, 187-188, 230
SFT NetWare, 7, 17, 217
Shareable, 85, 131
SHELL.CFG, 191
SHORT YEAR, 107
Show (flag), 48, 195
SHOWFILE, 94, 189, 230
SIZE, 131-132
SIZE GREATER THAN (flag), 131
SIZE NOT GREATER THAN (flag), 131
SIZE NOT LESS THAN (flag), 131
SLIST, 190, 230
SMACHINE, 106
SMODE, 191-192, 230
SORT, 131
SPOOL, 45, 47, 70, 72, 134, 146, 160, 162, 193-195, 197, 230
START, 25-26, 224
Start Batch File, 13
START PRINTER, 88, 98, 145, 153, 168, 194, 198, 230
STATION, 50, 106, 116
Station Number, 57
Statistics, 77
Status, 77
STOP PRINTER, 88, 153, 168, 198-199, 230
Subdirectory Information, 81
SUBST, 119
SUPERVISER, 217
SUPPRESS FORM FEED, 145
SYSCON, 33, 39-40, 55, 76, 89, 104, 108, 115, 165-166, 174, 187, 200-202, 205, 235, 240
SYSTEM, 4, 80, 131
System Command, 217
System Fault Tolerant, 4
System Login Script, 201
SYSTIME, 202, 230

**TAB SIZE**, 145
Tabs, 48, 134, 195
TIME, 186, 203-204, 230
Timeout, 48, 195
TIMEOUT COUNT, 146
Timer, 50
TLIST, 205-206, 230
Token Passing, 9, 217
Token Ring, 9, 233
Transaction Tracking System, 5, 77, 131
TROUBLESHOOTING, 29
Trustee Rights, 41, 79, 165, 209

**UDIR**, 130, 207, 230
Uninterruptable Power Supply, 7
UNIQUE PASSWORD, 117
UPDATE, 132
UPGRADE, 234
UPS, 222
UPS Monitoring, 7
User Information, 201
User List, 183
User Rights, 40
USERDEF, 239
USERLIST, 102, 183, 209-210, 213, 218, 230

**Version**, 77
VIEW, 111
VOLINFO, 55, 211-212, 230
Volume, 55, 211, 218
Volume Information, 81

**WHOAMI**, 213, 230
Wildcard, 218
Workgroup, 235
Workstation, 3, 7, 11, 31-32, 218, 222-234
Workstation Mode, 59, 66
Workstation Node Address, 116
Workstation Prompt, 218
Workstation RAM, 8
Workstation Shell, 27-28, 31, 223
WRITE, 89, 106, 170, 174, 205

**YEAR**, 107

# Other Books from Wordware Publishing, Inc.

### Artificial Intelligence
Illustrated VP-Expert

### Business-Professional Books
Business Emotions
The Business Side of Writing
Consulting Handbook for the High-Tech Professional
Hawks Do, Buzzards Don't
How to Win Pageants
Innovation, Inc.
Investor Beware
MegaTraits
Occupying the Summit
Steps to Strategic Management

### Computer Aided Drafting
Illustrated AutoCAD (Release 9)
Illustrated AutoCAD (Release 10)
Illustrated AutoCAD on the Mac II
Illustrated AutoLISP
Illustrated AutoSketch 1.04
Illustrated AutoSketch 2.0
Illustrated GenericCADD Level 3

### Database Management
The DataFlex Developer's Handbook
Illustrated dBASE II (2nd Ed.)
Illustrated dBASE III Plus
Illustrated dBASE IV
Illustrated Force 2.0
Illustrated FoxPro
llustrated Paradox 3.0 Volume II (2nd Ed.)

### Desktop Publishing
Achieving Graphic Impact with Ventura 2.0
Desktop Publisher's Dictionary
Handbook of Desktop Publishing
Illustrated PFS:First Publisher 2.0
Illustrated PageMaker 3.0
Illustrated Ready, Set, Go! 4.5 (Macintosh)
Illustrated Ventura 2.0
Ventura Troubleshooting Guide

### General Advanced Topics
Illustrated Dac Easy Accounting 3.0
Illustrated Dac Easy Accounting 4.1
Illustrated Harvard Graphics
Illustrated Novell NetWare 2.15
Novell NetWare: Adv. Tech. and Applications

### Integrated
Illustrated Enable/OA
Illustrated Framework III
Illustrated Microsoft Works 2.00
Illustrated Q & A 3.0 (2nd Ed.)

### Programming Languages
Illustrated C Programming (ANSI) (2nd Ed.)
Illustrated Clipper 5.0

### Programming Languages (cont.)
The DataFlex Developer's Handbook
The FOCUS Developer's Handbook
Graphic Programming with Turbo Pascal 5.5
Illustrated Turbo C++
Illustrated Turbo Pascal 4.0
Illustrated Turbo Pascal 5.5

### Spreadsheet
Illustrated Lotus 1-2-3 2.01
Illustrated Lotus 1-2-3 Rel. 3.0
Illustrated Lotus 1-2-3 Rel. 2.2
Illustrated Microsoft Excel 2.10 (IBM)
Illustrated Microsoft Excel 1.5 (Macintosh)
Illustrated Multiplan 2.0
Illustrated Quattro
Illustrated SuperCalc 5

### Systems and Operating Guides
Illustrated Microsoft Windows 2.0
Illustrated MS/PC DOS 3.3
Illustrated MS/PC DOS 4.0 (6th Ed.)
Illustrated UNIX

### Word Processing
Illustrated DisplayWrite 4
Illustrated Microsoft Word 5.0
Illustrated Microsoft Word for the Mac
Illustrated WordPerfect 1.0 (Macintosh)
Illustrated WordPerfect 4.2
Illustrated WordPerfect 5.0
Illustrated WordPerfect 5.1
Illustrated WordStar 3.3
Illustrated WordStar 6.0
Illustrated WordStar Professional (Rel. 5)
The New WordStar Customizing Guide 4.0
WordPerfect: Advanced Applications Handbook
WordPerfect Wizardry

### Popular Applications Series
Presentations with Harvard Graphics
Learn WordPerfect in a Day
Mailing Lists using dBASE
WordPerfect Macros

### Regional
Exploring the Alamo Legends
Forget the Alamo
The Great Texas Airship Mystery
100 Days in Texas: The Alamo Letters
Rainy Days in Texas Funbook
Texas Highway Humor
Texas Wit and Wisdom
That Cat Won't Flush
They Don't Have to Die
This Dog'll Hunt
Unsolved Texas Mysteries

Call Wordware Publishing, Inc. for names of the bookstores in your area
(214) 423-0090